GLOUCESTER
& THE FOREST OF DEAN

Aylburton	28	Longlevens	3
Beachley	38	Lower Tuffley	11
Berry Hill	17	Lydbrook	29
Bilson Green	33	Lydney	27
Blakeney	26	Maisemore	1
Bream	23	Mitcheldean	40
Broadwell	18	Newent	36
Brockworth	14	Newnham	35
Chepstow	37	Parkend	24
Churchdown	4	Quedgeley	10
Cinderford	34	Ruardean	30
City Centre	16	Ruardean Hill	31
Clearwell	19	Ruspidge	35
Coalway	20	Sedbury	37
Coleford	19	Sling	22
Coney Hill	7	St. Briavels	21
Drybrook	31	St. Pauls	5
Dymock	39	Staunton	40
Five Acres	17	Tredworth	6
Hardwicke	15	Tuffley	12
Highnam	9	Upton St. Leonards	13
Hucclecote	8	Westbury-on-Severn	32
Huntley	39	Yorkley	24
Kingsholm	2	Yorkley Slade	25

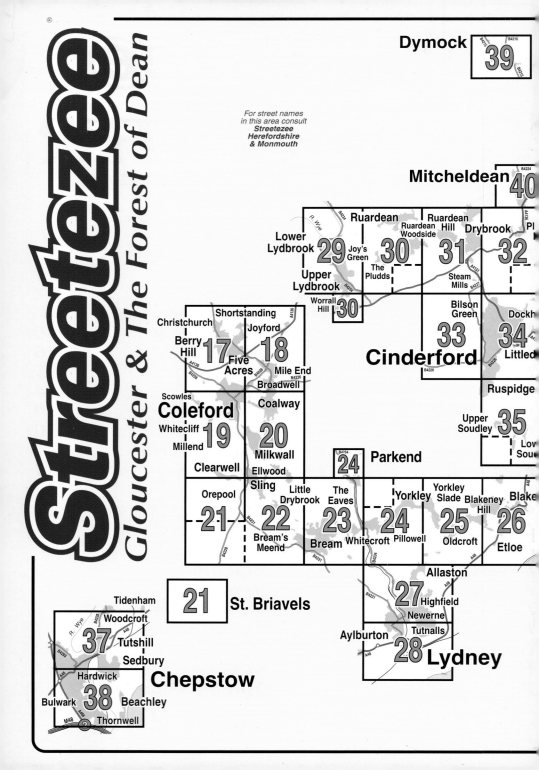

Streetezee

Gloucester & The Forest of Dean

Dymock **39**

For street names in this area consult *Streetezee Herefordshire & Monmouth*

Mitcheldean **40**

Lower Lydbrook **29** Joy's Green
Upper Lydbrook
Worrall Hill **30**
Ruardean
Ruardean Woodside **30**
The Pludds
Ruardean Hill **31**
Steam Mills
Drybrook **32**
Pl

Christchurch
Berry Hill
Shortstanding
Joyford **18**
17
Five Acres
Mile End
Broadwell

Bilson Green **33**
Dockh
34
Littled

Cinderford

Scowles
Coleford
Whitecliff
Millend **19**
Clearwell
Coalway **20**
Milkwall
Ellwood
Sling

Ruspidge

Upper Soudley **35**
Lov
Sou

Parkend **24**

Orepool **21**
Little Drybrook **22**
Bream's Meend
The Eaves **23**
Bream
Whitecroft

Yorkley **24**
Pillowell
Yorkley Slade **25**
Oldcroft
Blakeney Hill
Etloe
Blake **26**

21 St. Briavels

Allaston
Highfield **27**
Newerne
Tutnalls
Aylburton **28** Lydney

Tidenham
Woodcroft
Tutshill
Sedbury **37**
Hardwick
Bulwark **38** Beachley
Thornwell
Chepstow

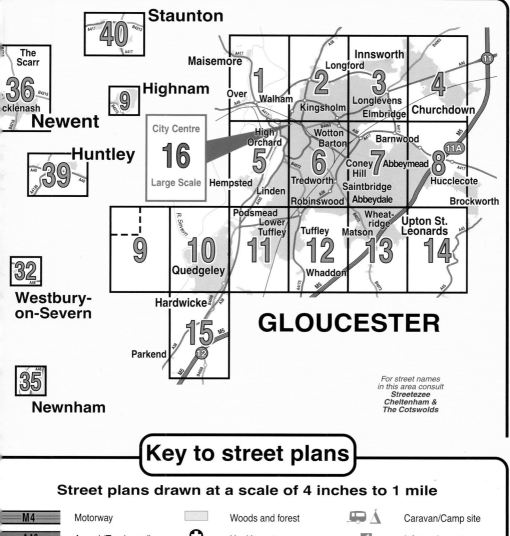

Staunton

40

The Scarr
36
cklenash

Newent

Highnam
9

Huntley
39

City Centre
16
Large Scale

32

Westbury-on-Severn

35

Newnham

Maisemore

1

Over **Walham**

High Orchard

5

Hempsted

Linden

Podsmead
Lower Tuffley

9

10

Quedgeley

11

Hardwicke

15

Parkend
12

Longford

Innsworth

2

3

Longlevens
Elmbridge

Kingsholm

Wotton Barton

6

Tredworth
Robinswood

Barnwood

Coney Hill
7 **Abbeymead**

Saintbridge
Abbeydale

Tuffley **Matson**

12

Whaddon

Churchdown

4

8 **Hucclecote**

Brockworth

Wheat-ridge

13

Upton St. Leonards
14

GLOUCESTER

For street names
in this area consult
Streetezee
Cheltenham &
The Cotswolds

Key to street plans

Street plans drawn at a scale of 4 inches to 1 mile

M4	Motorway	Woods and forest	Caravan/Camp site
A48	A road (Trunk road)	✚ Health centre	ℹ Information centre
B4281	B road	Petrol station	Picnic site
	Through road	✝ ✡ Places of worship	Golf course
	Dual carriageway	Police station	M Museum
	Track	✉ Post Office	Public house
	Footpath	☏ ☏ Telephone/Emergency	Theatre
	Railway	T Toilet facility	YHA Youth Hostel
	Urban area	P&R Park & Ride	House numbers
	Recreation ground	P Car parks (major)	H A&E Hospital/A&E

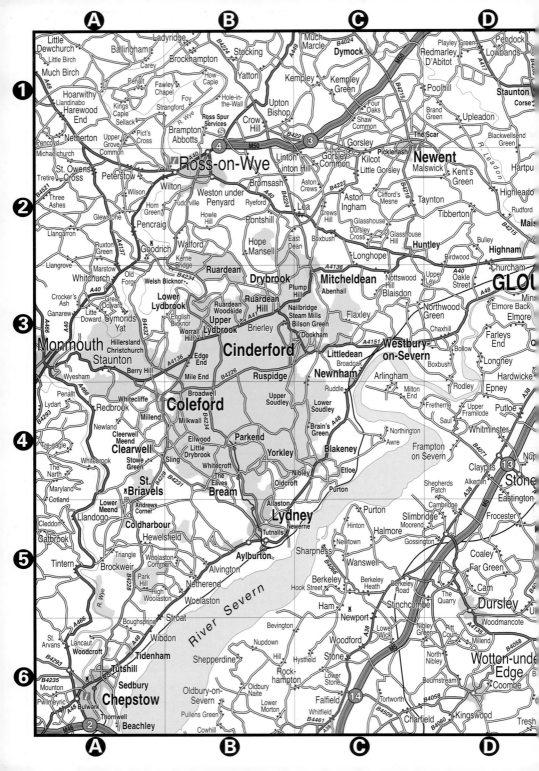

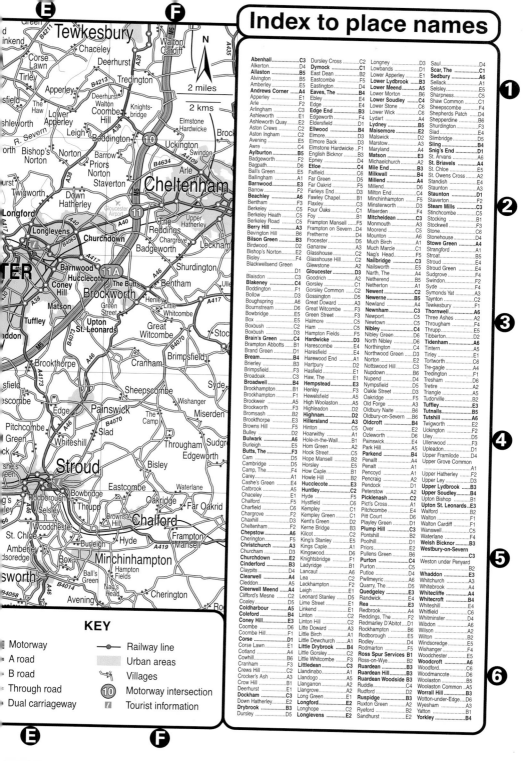

Index to place names

Abenhall	C3	Dursley Cross	C2	Longney	D3	Saul	D4
Alkerton	D4	Dymock	C1	Lowbands	D1	Scar, The	C1
Allaston	B5	East Dean	B3	Lower Apperley	E1	Sedbury	A6
Alvington	B5	Eastcombe	F5	Lower Lydbrook	B3	Sellack	A1
Amberley	A4	Eastington	D4	Lower Meend	A5	Selsley	E5
Andrews Corner	A4	Eaves, The	B4	Lower Morton	B6	Sharpness	C5
Apperley	E1	Ebley	E4	Lower Soudley	C4	Shaw Common	C1
Arle	F2	Edge	E4	Lower Stone	C6	Sheepscombe	F4
Arlingham	C3	Edge End	B3	Lower Wick	C6	Shepherds Patch	D4
Ashleworth	E1	Edgeworth	F4	Lydart	A4	Shepperdine	B6
Ashleworth Quay	E2	Eldersfield	D1	Lydney	B5	Shurdington	F3
Aston Crews	C2	Ellwood	B4	Maisemore	E2	Slad	E4
Aston Ingham	C2	Elmore	D3	Malswick	D2	Slimbridge	D5
Avening	E5	Elmore Back	D3	Marstow	A3	Sling	B4
Awre	A4	Elmstone Hardwicke	F1	Maryland	A4	Snig's End	D1
Aylburton	B5	English Bicknor	B3	Matson	E3	St. Arvans	A6
Badgeworth	F2	Epney	D3	Michaelchurch	A2	St. Briavels	A4
Bagpath	D6	Etloe	C4	Mile End	B3	St. Chloe	E5
Ball's Green	E5	Falfield	C6	Milkwall	B4	St. Owens Cross	A2
Ballingham	A1	Far Green	D5	Millend	A4	Standish	E4
Barnwood	E3	Far Oakrid	F5	Millend	D6	Staunton	A4
Barrow	F2	Farleys End	D3	Milton End	D3	Staunton	D1
Beachley	A6	Fawley Chapel	B1	Minchinhampton	F5	Staverton	F2
Bentham	F3	Flaxley	C3	Minsterworth	D3	Steam Mills	C3
Berkeley	C5	Four Oaks	B1	Miserden	F4	Stinchcombe	C5
Berkeley Heath	C5	Frampton Mansell	F5	Mitcheldean	C3	Stocking	B1
Berkeley Road	C5	Frampton on Severn	D4	Monmouth	A3	Stockwell	F3
Berry Hill	A3	Fretherne	D4	Moorend	C5	Stone	C6
Bevington Hill	B6	Frocester	D5	Mounton	A6	Stonehouse	D4
Bilson Green	B3	Ganarew	A3	Much Birch	A1	Stowe Green	A4
Birdwood	D2	Glasshouse	A2	Much Marcle	C1	Strangford	A1
Bishop's Norton	E2	Glasshouse Hill	C2	Nag's Head	F5	Stroat	B5
Bisley	F4	Glewstone	A2	Nailbridge	C3	Stroud	E4
Blackwellsend Green	D1	Gloucester	D3	Nailsworth	E5	Stroud Green	E4
Blaisdon	D2	Goodrich	A2	Narth, The	A4	Sudgrove	F4
Blakeney	C4	Gorsley	C1	Netherend	B5	Swindon	F2
Boddington	F1	Gorsley Common	C2	Netherton	A1	Syde	F4
Bollow	D3	Gossington	D5	Newent	C2	Symonds Yat	A3
Boughspring	A6	Great Doward	A3	Newerne	B5	Taynton	C2
Bournstream	D6	Great Witcombe	F3	Newland	B4	Tewkesbury	F1
Bowbridge	E5	Green Street	F3	Newnham	C3	Thornwell	A6
Box	F5	Halmore	C5	Newport	C5	Three Ashes	A2
Boxbush	C2	Ham	C5	Newtown	C5	Througham	F4
Boxbush	D3	Hampton Fields	F5	Nibley	C4	Thrupp	E5
Brain's Green	C4	Hardwicke	D3	Nibley Green	D6	Tibberton	D2
Brampton Abbotts	A2	Harescombe	E4	North Nibley	C6	Tidenham	A6
Brand Green	D1	Haresfield	E4	Northington	C4	Tintern	A5
Bream	B4	Harewood End	A1	Northwood Green	D3	Tirley	E1
Brierley	B3	Hartpury	D2	Norton	E2	Tortworth	C6
Brimpsfield	F3	Hasfield	E1	Nottswood Hill	C3	Tre-gagle	A4
Broadoak	D3	Haw, The	E1	Nupdown	B6	Tredington	F1
Broadwell	B4	Hempstead	E3	Nupend	C4	Tresham	D6
Brockhampton	B2	Henley	F3	Nympsfield	D5	Tretire	A2
Brockhampton	F1	Hewelsfield	A5	Oakle Street	D3	Triangle	E5
Brockweir	A5	High Woolaston	A5	Oakridge	F5	Tudorville	A2
Brockworth	F3	Highleadon	D2	Old Forge	A3	Tuffley	E3
Bromsash	B2	Highnam	D2	Oldbury Naite	B5	Tutnalls	B5
Brookthorpe	E3	Hillersland	A3	Oldbury-on-Severn	B6	Tutshill	A6
Browns Hill	E4	Hinton	C5	Oldcroft	B4	Twigworth	E2
Bulley	D2	Hoarwithy	A1	Over	E2	Uley	D5
Bulwark	A6	Hole-in-the-Wall	A1	Ozleworth	D6	Ullenwood	F2
Burleigh	E5	Hom Green	A2	Painswick	E4	Upleadon	D1
Butts, The	F3	Hook Street	C5	Park Hill	A5	Upper Framilode	D4
Cam	D5	Hope Mansell	B2	Parkend	B4	Upper Grove Common	A1
Cambridge	D5	Horsley	E5	Penallt	A4	Upper Hatherley	F2
Camp, The	F4	How Caple	B1	Penalt	A1	Upper Ley	D3
Carey	A1	Howle Hill	B2	Pencoyd	A1	Upper Lydbrook	B3
Cashe's Green	A4	Hucclecote	E3	Pencraig	A2	Upper Soudley	B4
Catbrook	A5	Huntley	C2	Pendock	D1	Upton Bishop	B1
Chaceley	E1	Hyde	F5	Peterstow	A2	Upton St. Leonards	E3
Chalford	F5	Hystfield	C5	Picklenash	C2	Walford	B2
Charfield	C6	Kempley	C1	Pict's Cross	A1	Walton	B2
Chargrove	F2	Kempley Green	C1	Pitchcombe	E4	Walton Cardiff	F1
Chaxhill	D2	Kent's Green	D2	Pitt Court	D6	Wanswell	C5
Cheltenham	F2	Kerne Bridge	B3	Playley Green	D1	Waterlane	F4
Chepstow	A6	Kilcot	C1	Plump Hill	C3	Welsh Bicknor	B3
Cherington	F5	King's Stanley	E5	Pontshill	B2	Westbury-on-Severn	C3
Christchurch	A3	Kingscote	D6	Poolhill	D1	Weston under Penyard	B2
Churcham	D3	Knightsbridge	F1	Priors	B2	Whaddon	E3
Churchdown	E2	Ladyridge	B1	Pullens Green	B6	Whitchurch	A3
Cinderford	B3	Lancaut	A6	Purton	C4	Whitebrook	A4
Claypits	D4	Lea	C2	Purton	C5	Whitecliffe	A4
Clearwell	A4	Leckhampton	F2	Putloe	D4	Whitecroft	B4
Cleddon	A5	Leigh	E1	Pwllmeyric	A6	Whiteshill	E4
Clifford's Mesne	C2	Leonard Stanley	E5	Quarry, The	D5	Whitfield	C6
Coaley	D5	Lime Street	E1	Quedgeley	E3	Whitminster	D4
Coldharbour	A5	Linkend	E1	Randwick	E4	Wibdon	A6
Coleford	B4	Linton	C2	Rea	E3	Wilson	A2
Coney Hill	C3	Linton Hill	C2	Redbrook	A4	Wilton	B2
Coombe	D6	Litte Doward	A3	Reddings, The	F2	Windsoredge	E5
Coombe Hill	F1	Little Birch	A1	Redmarley D'Abitot	D1	Wishanger	F4
Corse	D1	Little Dewchurch	A1	Rockhampton	B6	Woodchester	E5
Corse Lawn	E1	Little Drybrook	B4	Rodborough	E5	Woodcroft	A6
Cotland	A4	Little Gorsley	C1	Rodley	D4	Woodford	C6
Cowhill	B6	Little Whitcombe	F3	Rodmarton	F5	Woodmancote	D6
Cranham	F3	Littledean	C3	Ross Spur Services	B1	Woolaston	B5
Crews Hill	C2	Llandinabo	A1	Ross-on-Wye	A2	Woolaston Common	A5
Crocker's Ash	A3	Llandogo	A5	Ruardean	B3	Worrall Hill	B3
Crow Hill	B1	Llangarron	A1	Ruardean Hill	B3	Wotton-under-Edge	D6
Deerhurst	E1	Llangrove	A2	Ruardean Woodside	B3	Wyesham	A3
Dockham	C3	Long Green	E1	Ruddle	C4	Yatton	B1
Down Hatherley	E2	Longford	E2	Rudford	D2	Yorkley	B4
Drybrook	B3	Longhope	C2	Ruspidge	C3		
Dursley	D5	Longlevens	E2	Ruxton Green	A2		
				Ryeford	E4		
				Sandhurst	E2		

KEY

- Motorway
- A road
- B road
- Through road
- Dual carriageway
- Railway line
- Urban areas
- Villages
- Motorway intersection
- Tourist information

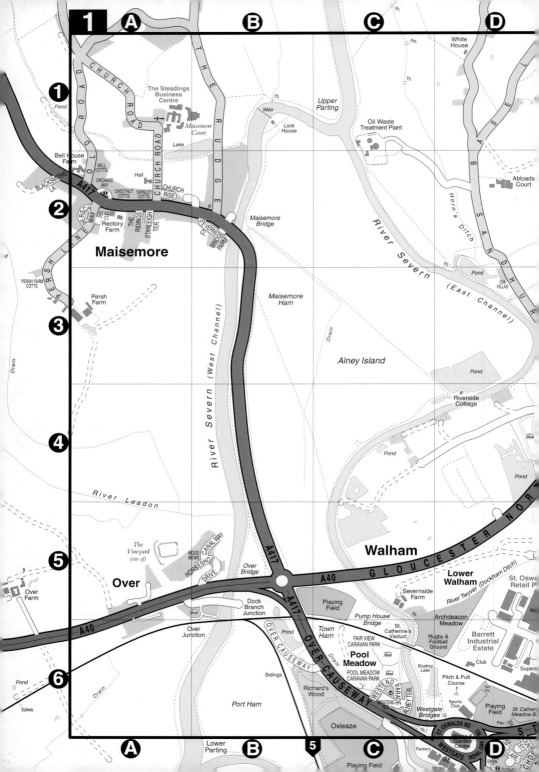

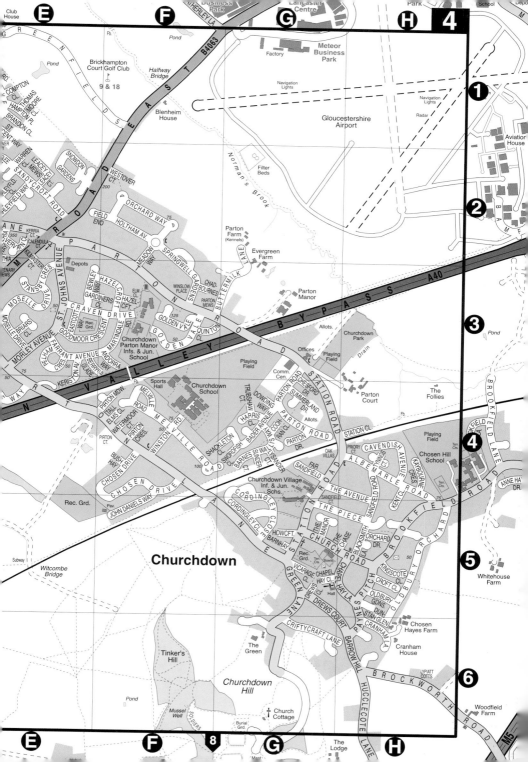

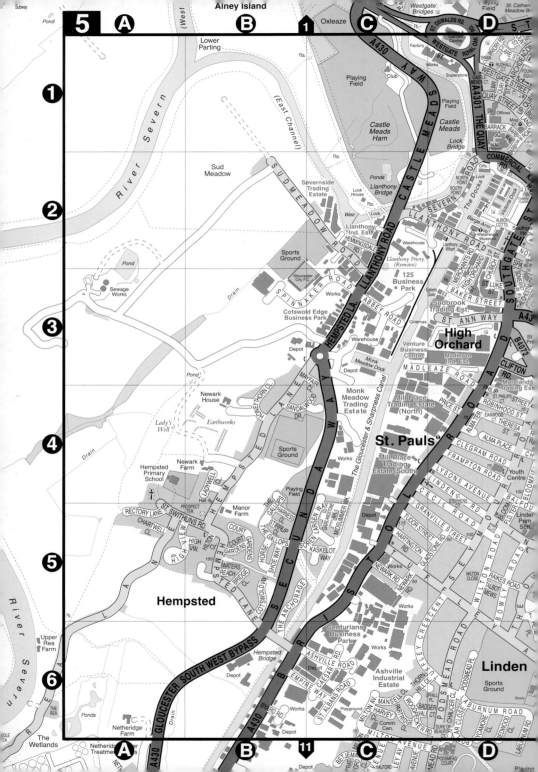

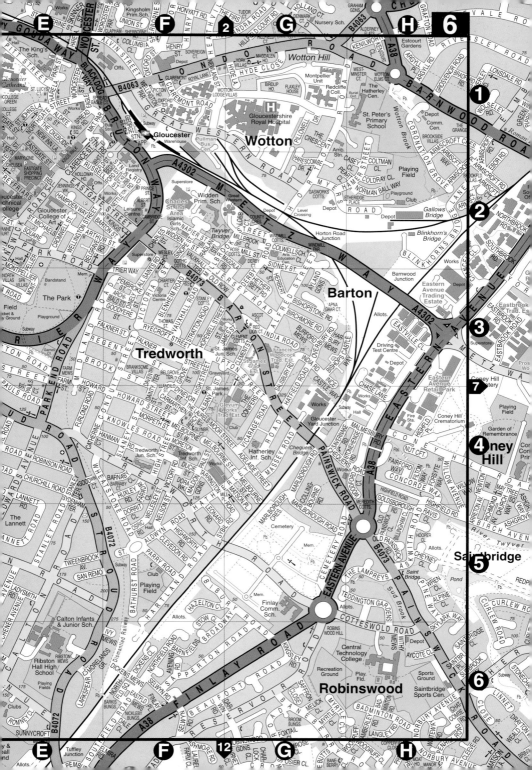

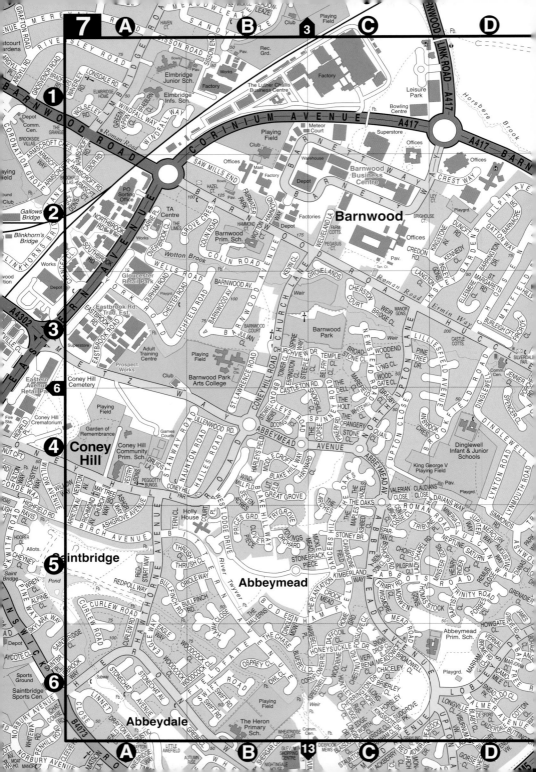

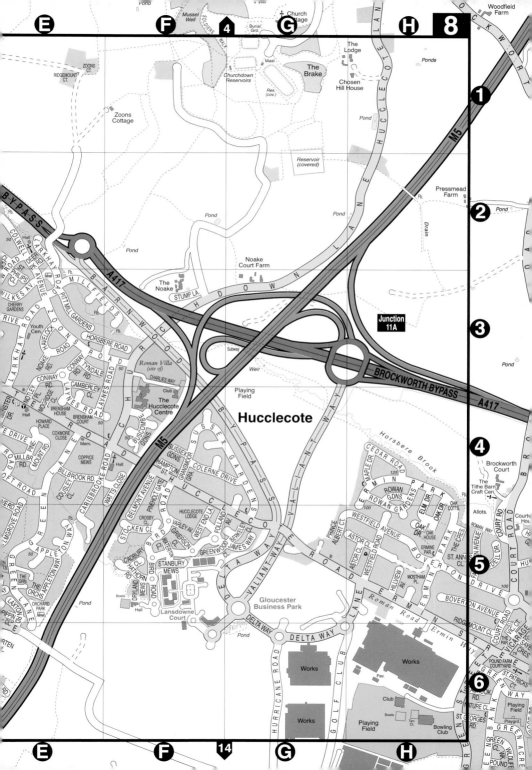

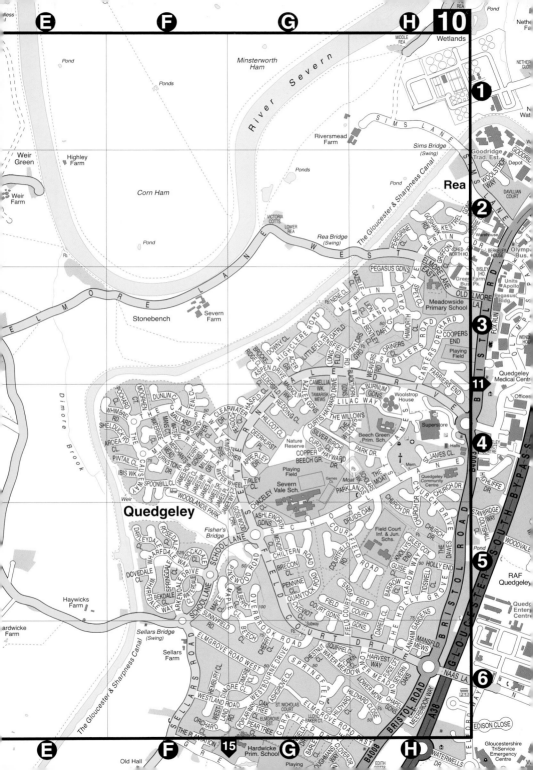

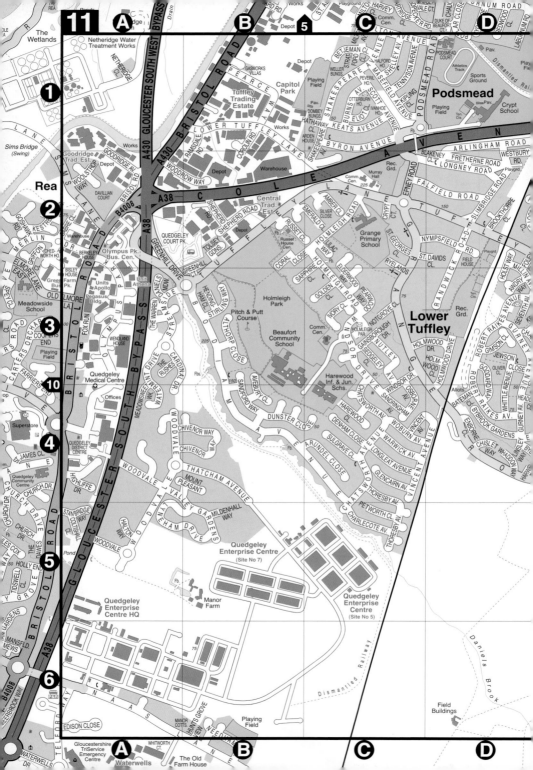

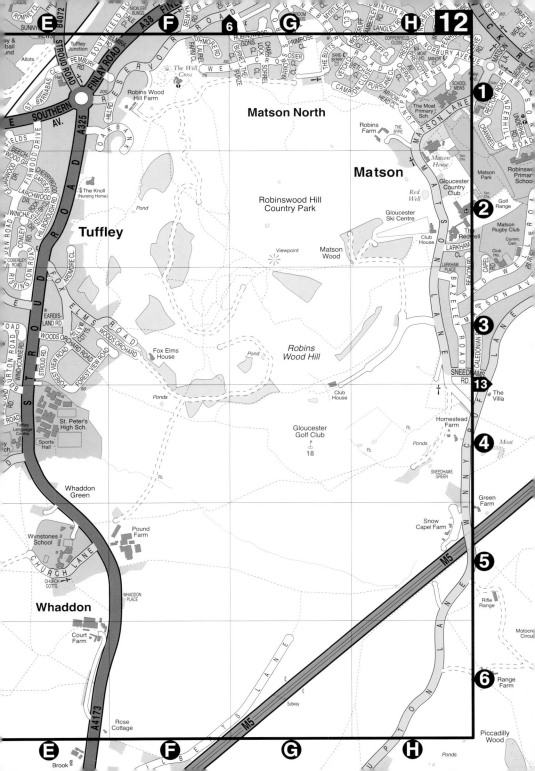

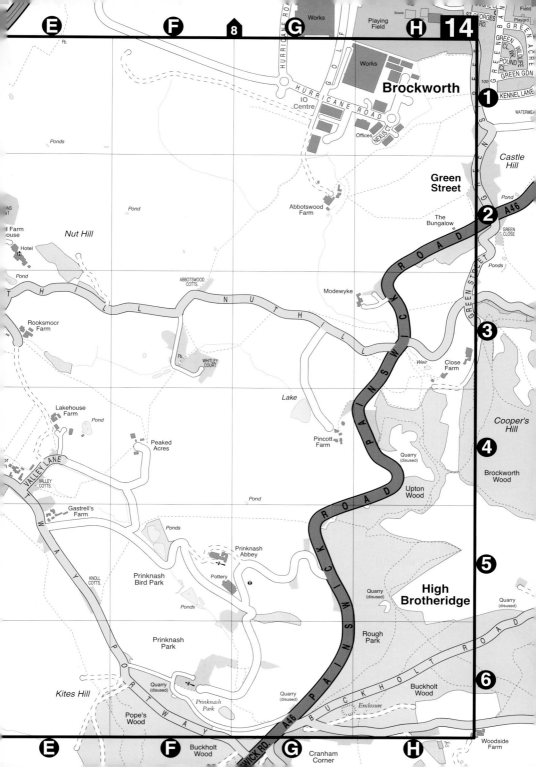

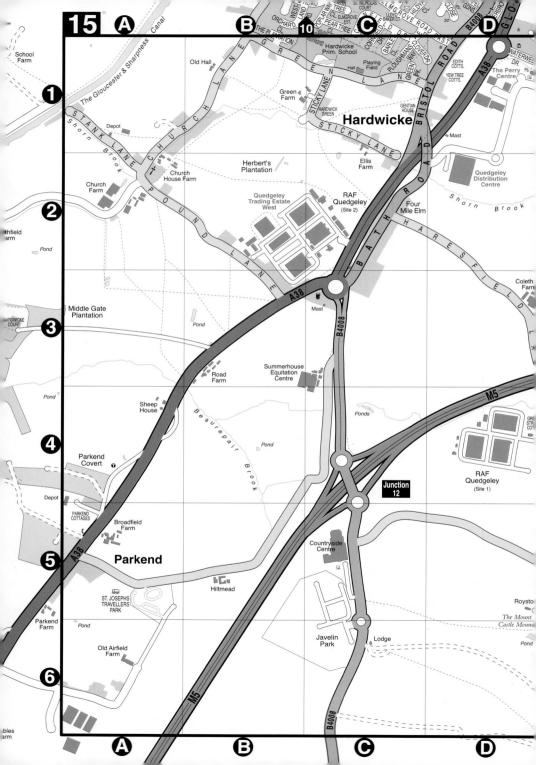

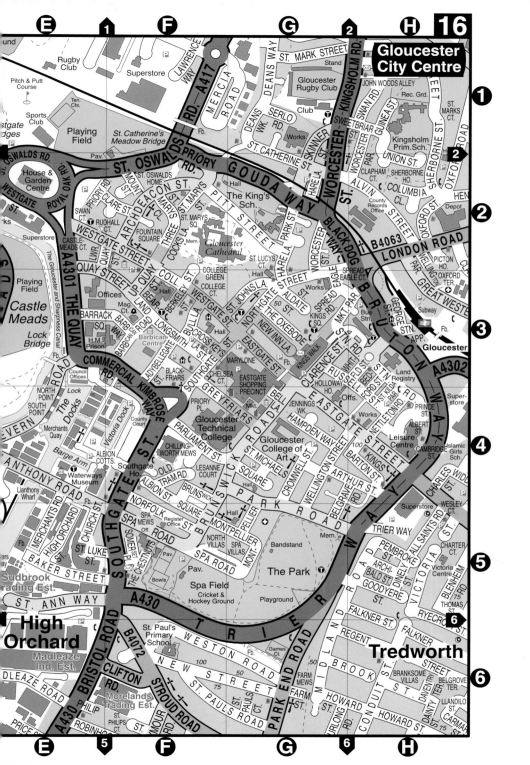

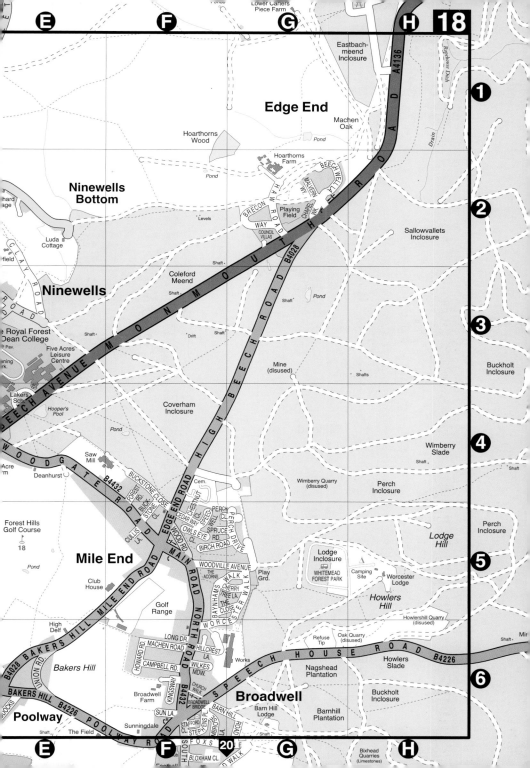

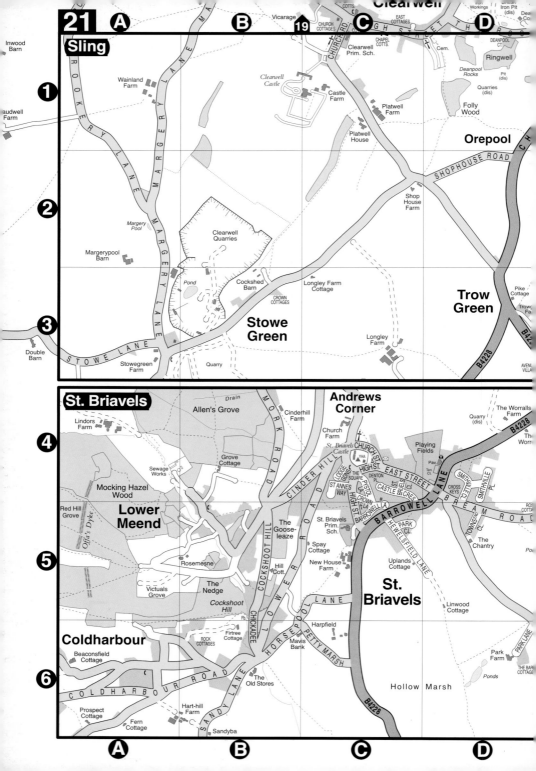

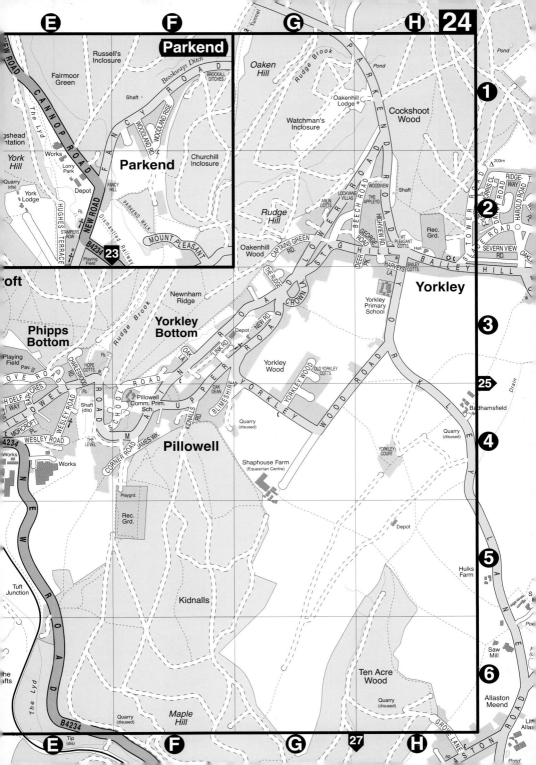

Parkend

Russell's Inclosure

Fairmoor Green

The Lyd

Brookways Ditch

BROCKALL DITCHES

Shaft

York Hill

Works

Lorry Park

Depot

Fancy Hill

FB

York Lodge

Quarry (dis)

STAMPERS ROW

HUGHES TERRACE

NEW ROAD

CANNOP ROAD

WOODLAND RISE

WOODLAND RD.

FANCY

Parkend

Churchill Inclosure

Parkend Walk

Dismantled Railway

MOUNT PLEASANT

B4234

23

Playing Field

Oaken Hill

Rudge Brook

PARKEND

Pond

Oakenhill Lodge

Watchman's Inclosure

Cockshoot Wood

Shaft

WOODVIEW

LOCKVANE VILLAS

THE APPLEYD

Rudge Hill

ARLIN COTTS.

HIGHVIEW RD.

MT. PLEASANT COTTS.

Rec. Grd.

Oakenhill Wood

CAPTAINS GREEN RD.

THE RIDGE

DEER PK.

GEORGE RD.

BEECH ROAD

STAG HILL

LOWER ROAD

HARVEYS

BAILEY COTTS.

BAILEY HILL

Hall

203m

RIDGEWAY

MORRIS CL.

HAROLD RD.

OAKL

SLADE ROAD

TOWER ROAD

SEVERN VIEW RD.

Yorkley

oft

Newnham Ridge

Rudge Brook

Phipps Bottom

Playing Field

Pav.

CHARLESWOOD RD.

HOPE COTTS.

PILLOWELL

GROVE ROAD

BARR CRES.

DELF WAY

MORCROFT PL.

WESLEY ROAD

B4234

N E W R O A D

Works

Works

THE LEVEL

Shaft (dis)

SCHOOL ROAD

CORNER ROAD

JAMES WK.

M

Playgrd.

Rec. Grd.

Pillowell

Pillowell Comm. Prim. Sch.

BLIMESHIRE

KIDNALLS

OAK DEAN

OAK

LINK RD.

UPPER ROAD

NEW RD.

Depot

CROWN LA.

ROAD

Yorkley Bottom

Yorkley Primary School

Yorkley Wood

Old Yorkley Cotts.

YORKLEY WOOD

WOOD ROAD

YORKLEY ROAD

Quarry (disused)

YORKLEY COURT

Shaphouse Farm (Equestrian Centre)

Kidnalls

Tuft Junction

The Lyd

B4234

Quarry (disused)

Maple Hill

Ten Acre Wood

Quarry (disused)

Depot

BAILEY LANE

Badhamsfield

Quarry (disused)

Hulks Farm

Saw Mill

Allaston Meend

GROVE LANE

ALLASTON ROAD

Lit Allas

50

Pond

The ifts

Tip (dis)

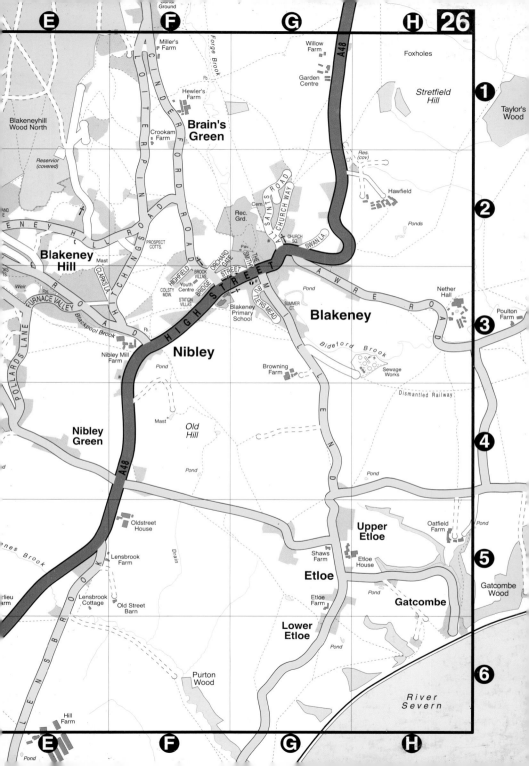

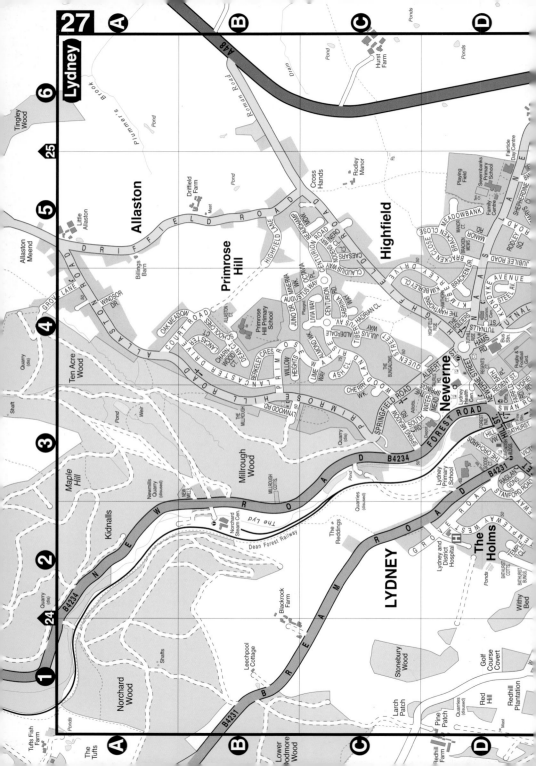

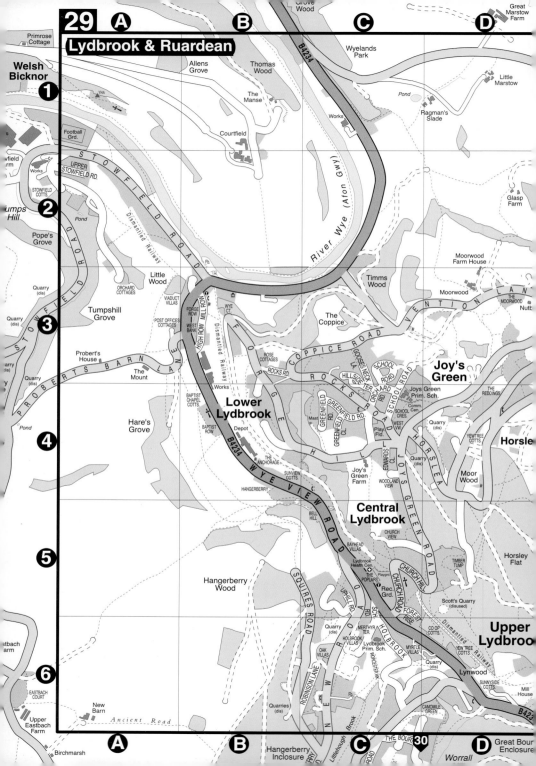

1
2
3
4
5
6

Welsh Bicknor

Primrose Cottage

YHA

Football Grd.

STOWFIELD ROAD

UPPER STOWFIELD RD.

STOWFIELD COTTS.

Pond

Pope's Grove

umps Hill

Quarry (dis)

Quarry (dis)

ield Farm

Works

Tumpshill Grove

ORCHARD COTTAGES

Little Wood

VIADUCT VILLAS

POST OFFICES COTTAGES

Probert's House

PROBERTS BARN LANE

The Mount

Hare's Grove

Pond

Allens Grove

Thomas Wood

The Manse

Courtfield

Grove Wood

B4234

Wyelands Park

Works

Pond

Ragman's Slade

Little Marstow

Great Marstow Farm

River Wye (Afon Gwy)

Moorwood Farm House

Glasp Farm

Dismantled Railway

Fb

ROSE COTTAGES

ROCKS RD.

FORGE ROW

HIGH ROW

WEST BANK

WYE CT.

MILL ROW

FORGE HILL

Dismantled Railway

Works

BAPTIST CHAPEL COTTS.

BAPTIST ROW

Lower Lydbrook

Depot

B4234

THE ANCHORAGE

SUNVIEW COTTS.

HANGERBERRY

BELL HILL

WYE VIEW ROAD

Joy's Green Farm

Timms Wood

The Coppice

COPPICE ROAD

GOOSES NECK

ORCHARD

SCHOOL ROAD

LA.

HILLSIDE

ROCKS RD.

GREENFIELD RD.

GREENFIELD CL.

Mast

School Cres.

Comm School Cen.

WEST VW.

Play Fld.

SCHOOL CRES.

Joys Green Prim. Sch.

Joy's Green

Moorwood

CONVENTION LANE

THE MOORWOOD

Nutb

THE REDDINGS

YEWTREE COTTS.

Horsle

Moor Wood

Quarry (dis)

Quarry (dis)

EDWARDS CL.

WOODLAND VIEW

HORSLEA

JOY'S GREEN ROAD

Central Lydbrook

CHURCH VIEW

BAYHEAD VILLAS

Lydbrook Health Cen.

THE POPLARS

Playgrd

Rec. Grd.

CHURCH ROAD

CHURCH HILL

CHURCH RISE

FOREST

Horsley Flat

TIMBER TUMP

Scott's Quarry (disused)

CO OP COTTS.

Hangerberry Wood

SQUIRES ROAD

UPHILL RD.

SCH.

HOLBROOK RD.

Quarry (dis)

HOLBROOK VILLAS

MERTHYR TER.

Lydbrook Prim. Sch.

WORCESTER VW.

MYRTLE VILLAS

Dismantled Railway

YEW TREE COTTS.

Lynwood

SUNNYSIDE COTTS.

Mill House

Upper Lydbroo

stbach arm

EASTBACH COURT

Upper Eastbach Farm

New Barn

Ancient Road

Birchmarsh

ROBINSON LANE

NEW

Quarries (dis)

OAK VILLAS

Littlehough Brook

CAMOMILE GREEN

THE BOUR

Worrall

B423

B4234

Hangerberry Inclosure

Great Bour Enclosure

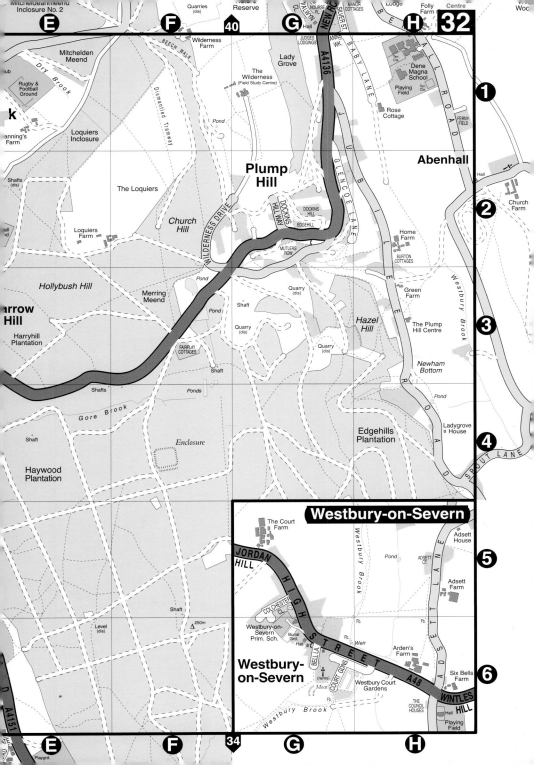

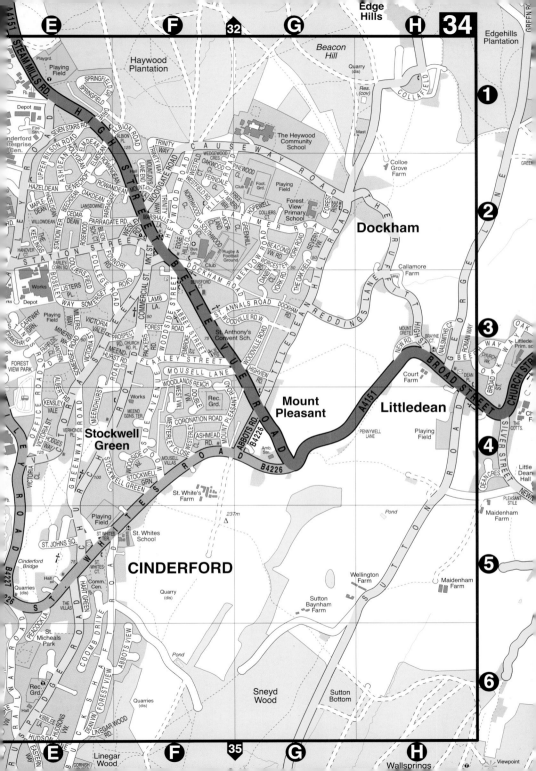

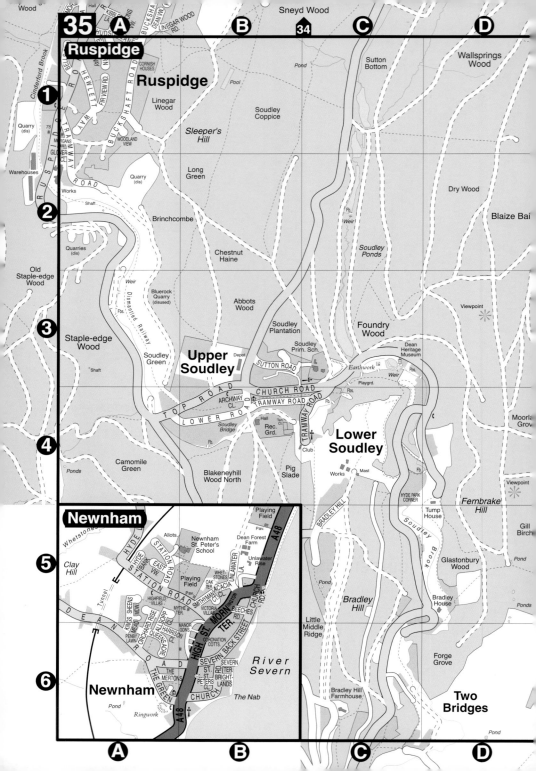

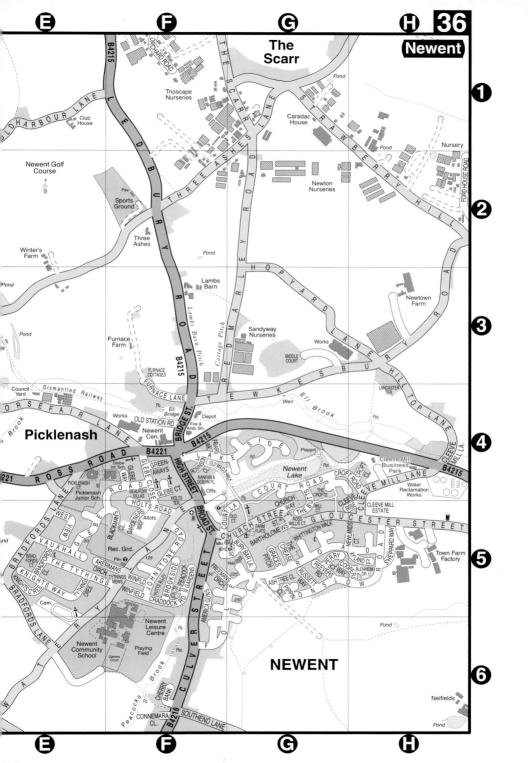

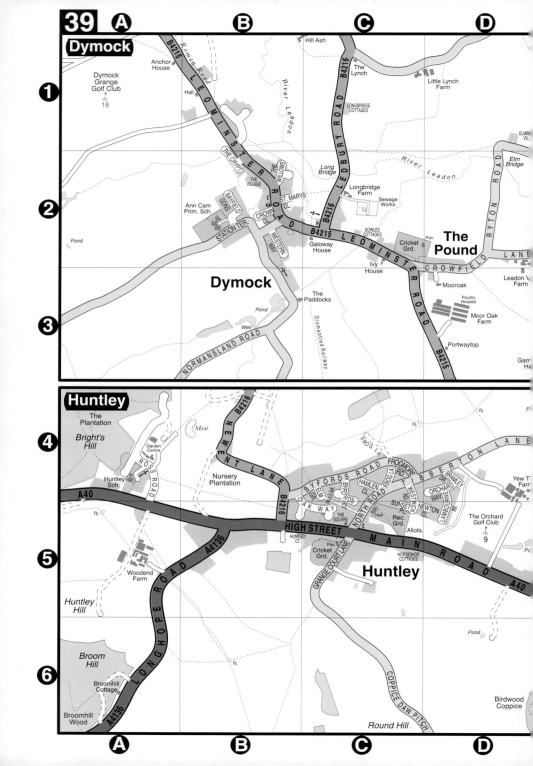

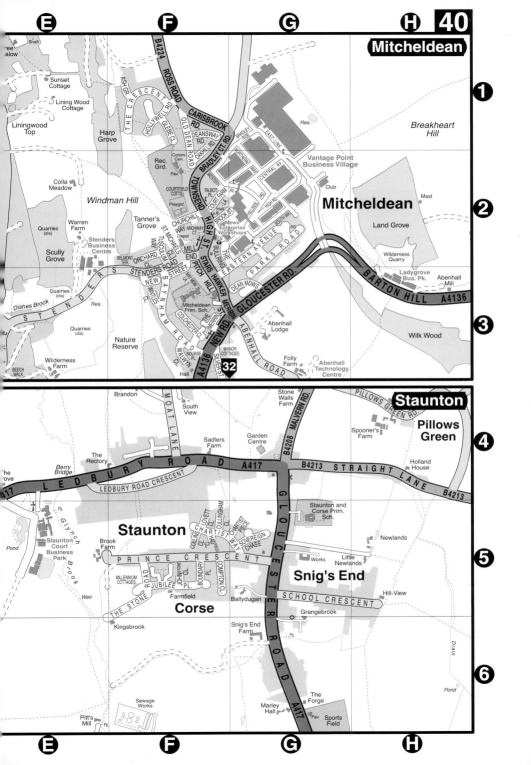

INDEX Abbreviations used

Allot(s).	Allotment(s)	Coll.	College	Fld(s).	Field(s)	Inf.	Infant	Off(s).	Office(s)	S.	South
Amb.	Ambulance	Comm.	Community	Flts.	Flats	Junc.	Junction	Orch(s).	Orchard(s)	Sq.	Square
App.	Approach	Comp.	Comprehensive	Fb(s).	Footbridge(s)	Jun.	Junior	Par.	Parade	Stn.	Station
Arc.	Arcade	Cov.	Covered	Gdns.	Gardens	La.	Lane	Pk.	Park	St.	Street
Av.	Avenue	Crn.	Corner	Gt.	Great	Lib.	Library	Pass.	Passage	Ten.	Tennis
Br.	Bridge	Cott(s).	Cottage(s)	Gra.	Grange	Lit.	Little	Pav.	Pavilion	Ter.	Terrace
Brd.	Broad	Cres.	Crescent	Grn.	Green	Lwr.	Lower	Pl.	Place	Up.	Upper
Bldg(s).	Building(s)	Cft.	Croft	Grd.	Ground	Mkt.	Market	Pr.	Precinct	Vic.	Vicarage
Bung(s).	Bungalow(s)	Ct.	Court	Gr.	Grove	Mag.	Magistrates	Prim.	Primary	Vw.	View
Bus.	Business	Dis.	Disused	Hd.	Head	Mdw(s).	Meadow(s)	Rec.	Recreation	Vlls.	Villas
Cara.	Caravan	Dr.	Drive	Hts.	Heights	Mem.	Memorial	Res.	Reservoir	Wk.	Walk
Cem.	Cemetery	E.	East	Hosp.	Hospital	Mon.	Monument	Resid.	Residential	Wy.	Way
Cen.	Centre	Ent.	Enterprise	Ho.	House	Mt.	Mount	Rd.	Road	W.	West
Cl.	Close	Est.	Estate	Ind.	Industrial	N.	North	Sch.	School	Yd.	Yard

Use of this Index:

1. An alphabetical order is followed.
2. Each street name is followed by a map reference giving a page number and coordinates: Abbey Road **5** C3.
3. Where a street name appears more than once the reference is given: Barnwood Bypass **7** D2/**8** E2.
4. Names not appearing on the map are shown with an * and the reference of the nearest adjoining street: Cathedral Court*, London Road **6** G1.
5. House numbers along streets are shown: *250*.

A

Abbey Road **5** C3
Abbey Street **34** F3
Abbey View*, Matson Av. ..**13** A1
Abbeydale Court **13** C1
Abbeyfield House*, London Rd.
.....................................**16** H2
Abbeymead Avenue
.....................**7** B4/C5/**13** C1
Abbots Road (Cinderford)..**34** G4
Abbots Road (Glos.) **7** C5
Abbots View.....................**34** F6
Abbotswood Close **11** D2
Abbotswood Cottages **14** F3
Abenhall Road **40** G3
Acacia Close (Bream) **23** B5
Acacia Close (Newnham) ..**35** B5
Acer Grove **10** G3
Acorn Court.....................**13** A1
Acorns, The **18** F5
Adams Way **17** C4
Adelaide Street **6** G4
Admirals Close **23** B4
Adsett Court **32** H5
Adsett Lane **32** F2
Aisne Road **25** B4
Akermans Orchard **36** E5
Albany Street....................**6** F4
Albemarle Road..................**4** H4
Albert Road (Cinderford) ..**34** E4
Albert Road (Coleford) **19** C1
Albert Street (Glos.)..........**16** H4
Albert Street (Lydney) **27** D4
Albion Cottages **16** E4
Albion Place.....................**34** F1
Albion Road **34** E3
Albion Square **37** D2
Albion Street **16** F4
Alder Close **3** A5
Alderdale **27** C4
Alderney Flats **2** H6
Alderney House*,Kenilworth Av.
....**6** H1
Alders Green **2** H4
Alderton Close.................**13** C1
Alexandra Road (Chepstow)
.....................................**38** F3
Alexandra Road (Glos.)........**2** G6
Alfred Street **6** G3
Alice Crescent **38** H4
Alington Close*, Derby Rd. ..**6** G2
All Saints Road (Blakeney) **26** G2
All Saints Road (Glos.) **16** H5
Allaston Court **27** B4
Allaston Road **27** A4
Allendale Close **3** A5
Allsopp Close...................**35** A6
Alma Drive......................**38** H4
Alma Place **5** D4
Alma Terrace **5** D4
Almond Close **13** B2
Almond Walk **27** C4
Almshouses*, East St.......**21** C4
Alney Terrace **1** C6
Alpha Road **38** F3
Alpine Close **6** H5
Althorp Close **11** B3
Alvin Street **16** H2
Amber Close **11** C2
Amberley Road **6** H6
Ambrose Lane **18** F6
America Gardens **36** F6
Anbrook Crescent **7** C4
Anchorage, The (Glos.) **5** B6
Anchorage, The (Lydbrook)
.....................................**29** B4
Andorra Way **4** F3
Angel Field **19** C1
Angelica Way **7** D6
Anne Edwards Mews*,
The Wheatridge **13** B1
Anne Hathaway Drive **4** H4
Anns Walk **32** G1
Ansdell Drive **8** H5
Apna Ghar Court **6** G3
Apperley Drive..................**10** G4
Apple Tree Close................**4** E2
Appleton Way **8** E5
Appletree Close...............**13** C1
Appleyard, The **24** H2
Apprentice Close **38** H5
Aragon Way......................**3** D2
Archdeacon Court*, Mount Street
.....................................**16** F2
Archdeacon Street **16** F2
Archibald Street...............**16** H5
Archway Close.................**35** B4
Archway Court **40** F2
Ardea Close.....................**10** E4
Arden House **11** B1
Ardmore Close.................**12** E3
Argyll Place **6** H1
Argyll Road **6** H1
Arkendale Drive **10** F5
Arlin Cottages **24** G2
Arlingham Road................**11** D1
Arlington Court **37** D5
Armada Close **3** D2
Armscroft Court **7** A2
Armscroft Crescent **6** H1
Armscroft Gardens **6** H2
Armscroft Place **6** H2
Armscroft Road **7** A2
Armscroft Way **6** H1
Arreton Avenue **7** A5
Arrowhead Close..............**12** H1
Arthur Cooper Way **19** D3
Arthur Street **16** G4
Arundel Close **11** C4
Ascot Court **6** G3
Ash Close (Chepstow) **38** G2
Ash Close (Lydney) **27** C4
Ash Grove (Glos.) **13** C2
Ash Grove (Mitchedean) **40** F1
Ash Grove Place **25** A3
Ash Path, The **13** C2
Ash Tree Close **36** G5
Ashbed Close **7** C5
Ashcroft Close **13** B3
Ashdean **34** E2
Ashdene Road **30** F4
Ashfield Cottages **38** E2
Ashfield Road..................**31** B3
Ashgrove Avenue **7** A5
Ashgrove Close................**10** G6
Ashgrove Way **7** A4
Ashleworth Gardens **10** G5
Ashmead **2** H4
Ashmead Road **34** F4
Ashmore Road..................**12** F1
Ashton Close **13** C2
Ashville Road **5** C6
Ashwood Way **7** D5
Askwith Road **6** H5
Aspen Drive **10** G3
Aston Bridge Road............**30** F4
Aston Close......................**17** D4
Astor Close **8** H5
Augustine Way **7** D5
Augustus Way **27** B4
Aust Crescent **38** G3
Austin Drive **2** F3
Autumn Rise **13** A1
Avebury Road **11** B3
Avening Road **6** F6
Avenue Andre Clement **28** G3
Avenue Villas **21** D3
Avenue, The (Churchdown) **4** G4
Avenue, The (Glos.) **3** A5
Avon House*, Shakespeare Av.
.....................................**11** C1
Awdry Way **11** D3
Awebridge Way **13** A1
Awre Road **26** G3
Aycote Close **6** H6
Ayland Close **36** H5
Ayland Gardens **6** G3
Azalea Gardens **10** G3

B

Baby Lane **32** G1
Back Lane **31** C1
Back Street **35** B6
Back, The **37** C3
Bader Avenue **4** G4
Badger Close **13** B2
Badger Vale Court..............**5** C6
Badgers Dene **38** E1
Badgers Way **23** B4
Badminton Road **6** H6
Badminton Villas **37** C3
Bailey Cottages **24** H2
Bailey Hill........................**24** H2
Baker Street.....................**16** E5
Bakers Hill **18** E6
Bakers Piece Road **30** H3
Balfour Road **5** D4
Ballinska Mews **3** B4
Bamfurlong Lane **4** H2
Baneberry Court **12** G1
Baneberry Road **6** G6

Bank Square 37 D2
Bank Street (Chepstow) 37 D2
Bank Street (Coleford)........19 D1
Baptist Chapel Cottages 29 B4
Baptist Close 7 D5
Baptist Way 31 B3
Barbican Centre.....16 F3
Barbican Road.....16 F3
Barbican Way 16 F3
Barkis Bungalows 6 F6
Barley Close 15 C1
Barleycorn Square.....34 E2
Barleycroft Close 13 B3
Barn Close.....13 C1
Barn Cottages, The 21 D6
Barn Ground 9 B1
Barn Hill Road 18 F6
Barn Lane 30 G3
Barnaby Close 6 F4
Barnaby Court 6 F4
Barnacre Drive 7 D2
Barnes Cottages 38 E5
Barnes Wallis Way 4 G4
Barnett Way 7 B2
Barnfields.....6 F6
Barnhay.....4 G5
Barnwood Avenue 7 B3
Barnwood Bypass.......7 D2/8 E2
Barnwood Court.....7 B3
Barnwood Link Road 3 C5
Barnwood Road 6 H1/7 B2
Barrack Square 16 E3
Barrington Drive 7 D2
Barrow Close.....10 H5
Barrow Hill.....4 H6
Barrowell Lane 21 C5
Barton Hill 40 H3
Barton Street 6 F3
Base Lane 1 D2
Basil Close.....13 B1
Bateman Close 11 D4
Bath Crescent 24 E4
Bath Place (Berry Hill).......12 H3
Bath Place (Lydney) 27 D4
Bath Road 15 C2
Bathurst Bungalows 27 D2
Bathurst Cottages 27 D2
Bathurst Park Road.....27 D3
Bathurst Road 6 F5
Batts Lane 31 B2
Bay Tree Road 7 D6/8 E6
Bayberry Place 20 F2
Bayfield Gardens 39 B2
Bayhead Villas.....29 C5
Baynham Road 40 F3
Baynhams Walk.....18 F5
Bazeley Road 12 H3
Beachley Road (Beachley) 38 F5
Beachley Road (Sedbury)
.....37 C3/D4
Beacon Road.....12 H3
Beacons View Road 34 G2
Bearland 16 F3
Beauchamp Meadow.....27 C5
Beaufort Buildings*, Spa Road
.....16 F5
Beaufort Drive 28 E4
Beaufort House*, Brunswick Rd.
.....16 F5
Beaufort Place.....37 D3
Beaufort Road 6 F6
Beaufort Square 37 D2
Beaufort Villas 36 F4

Beaumont Place 28 E3
Beaumont Road.....3 A4
Beckford Road.....13 C1
Beckside Court*, Millbrook St.
.....6 G2
Bedford Street 16 H3
Beech Avenue 18 E4
Beech Close (Glos.) 10 G6
Beech Close (Highnam) 9 A2
Beech Grove 38 E1
Beech Road (Yorkley) 24 H2
Beech Road*, Forest View Park
.....34 E4
Beech Walk 32 F1/40 E3
Beech Way (Bream) 23 B5
Beech Way (Littledean).....34 H3
Beech Well Lane.....18 G2
Beechcroft Road 2 G4
Beechdean 34 E2
Beeches Road.....35 B5
Beechwood Grove.....12 E1
Bekdale Close 10 F5
Belfry Close 7 C3
Belfry, The 38 E6
Belgrave Road 16 G5
Belgrove Terrace 16 H6
Bell Cottages 1 A2
Bell Lane (Glos.) 16 G4
Bell Lane (Westbury).....32 G6
Belle Vue Road (Cinderford)
.....34 F2
Belle Vue Road (Ruardean)
.....30 G1
Bellevue Cottages 23 B4
Bells Court 20 E4
Bells Place (Coleford) 19 D1
Bells Place (Ruspidge) 35 A1
Belmont Avenue 8 F5
Belmont Lane 17 D3
Belmont Terrace 40 F2
Ben Hill 29 C5
Benson Close 7 C5
Bentley Close 10 H3
Berisford Court.....31 F3
Berisford Court*, Dockham Road
.....34 F2
Berkeley Close 8 G5
Berkeley Crescent 27 B4
Berkeley House 11 A2
Berkeley Street 16 F3
Berry Lawn 13 B2
Berryfield Glade.....4 E3
Bessemer Close 19 D2
Betjeman Close 11 C1
Bewley Way.....4 E3
Bibury Road 6 F5
Bicknor Street 17 D2
Bigstone Close 37 C4
Bigstone Grove 37 C3
Bijou Court.....2 F5
Bilberry Close 13 D1
Billbrook Road 8 E4
Billingham Close 6 H5
Bilson School Court.....34 E2
Birch Avenue 7 A5
Birch Park 20 F2
Birch Road.....18 F5
Birchall Avenue 13 A3
Birchmore Road 6 G3
Birchwood Close 33 D2
Birchwood Fields.....11 D2
Bird Road.....8 F5
Birdlip House 6 G1

Birdwood Close 13 C1
Bishops Castle Way 6 G3
Bishops Close 38 H3
Bishops Gate.....28 E3
Bishops Road 7 C5
Bishopstone Road.....6 G3
Bishton Lane 37 A4/A5
Bisley House 11 A3
Bisley Road 12 E4
Bittern Avenue 7 A5
Bixhead Walk.....20 F1
Black Dog Way 16 G2
Blackberry Close 13 C1
Blackbird Avenue.....3 B3
Blackfriars.....16 F3
Blackmans Close 36 F5
Blacksmith Lane (Churchdown)
.....4 H5
Blacksmiths Ground 9 B1
Blacksmiths Lane (Maisemore)
.....1 A2
Blackthorn Gardens.....10 H3
Blackwater Way.....3 C4
Blaisdon Close 13 C1
Blake Hill Way 7 B4
Blakeley Court.....3 D3
Blakeney Close 11 C2
Blakeney Hill Road 25 D2
Blenheim Drive 36 H5
Blenheim House*,
    Hucclecote Road 8 F4
Blenheim Road 16 H5
Blimeshire 24 F4
Blinkhorns Bridge Lane 6 H2
Bloomfield Road 5 D4
Bloomfield Terrace 5 D5
Bloxham Close.....20 F1
Blue Rock Crescent.....23 B4
Bluebell Close (Glos.) 7 B6
Bluebell Close (Milkwall) 20 F4
Bluebell Drive 38 G3
Bodenham Field 7 B5
Bodiam Avenue 11 B3
Bohanam House*, Barnwood Rd.
.....6 H1
Boleyn Close 3 D2
Bondend Road.....13 C3/D2
Borage Close.....7 D6
Boseley Row 31 D2
Boseley Way 34 E3
Boundary Place 40 F5
Bourton Road 12 E4
Bourts, The 29 C6
Boverton Avenue.....8 H5
Boverton Drive.....8 H5
Bowens Hill 19 C1
Bowens Hill Road 19 C1
Bowly Road 5 D5
Bowson Road 23 B3
Bowson Square 23 B4
Box Tree Close 30 G1
Boxbush Road.....19 C1
Boxtree Cottages 30 G1
Boyce Close 13 C2
Bracelands Drive 17 B3
Bracken Close 27 D5
Bracken Drive 27 D4
Bracken Mews.....27 D5
Bracken Road 31 D1
Bradford Road.....6 H1
Bradfords Close 36 E5
Bradfords Court 36 E5

Bradfords Lane 36 E5
Bradley Close 3 A5
Bradley Court Road 40 F2
Bradley Hill 35 C5
Bradley Rise 40 G1
Bradshaw Close 3 C4
Brae Walk 13 B1
Braeburn Close 7 A1
Bramble Lawn 13 B2
Bramble Road 20 E4
Bramley Drive 39 D4
Bramley Mews 8 E5
Branch, The.....31 D4
Brandon Close.....4 E1
Branksome Villas.....16 G6/H6
Brasenose Cottages 2 G1
Brayne Court 34 H3
Bream Avenue.....22 E4
Bream Road (Lydney) 27 B1
Bream Road (St. Briavels)..21 D4
Brecon Close.....10 G5
Brecon Way.....18 G2
Brehal Close 28 E3
Breinton Way 3 B4
Brensham Court 8 E4
Brensham House.....8 E4
Briar Cottages 31 B2
Briar Lawn 13 B2
Briars Close 4 E3
Bridge Close 5 B5
Bridge Farm.....1 B2
Bridge Road 31 C3
Bridge Street (Blakeney) ...26 F3
Bridge Street (Chepstow) .37 C2
Bridge Street (Newent) 36 F4
Bridget Drive 38 E4
Brierley Close 7 C6
Brierley Road.....30 H3
Brierley Way 25 B4
Brighouse Court 7 C2
Brightlands.....35 B6
Brimsome Meadow 9 B1
Brindle Close 13 A1
Brionne Way 2 H4
Bristol Road (Glos.)
.....11 A1/A4/16 E6
Bristol Road (Hardwicke)
.....10 H6/15 C1
Briton Close.....38 H4
Broad Leys Road.....7 B3
Broad Street (Littledean)
.....34 H3/H4
Broad Street (Newent) 36 F5
Broadmoor Park 31 D6
Broadmoor Road.....31 D6
Broadstone Close 7 C3
Broadway.....6 F6
Broadwell Bridge 18 F6
Broadwell Close 7 C6
Brockall Ditches.....24 F1
Brockeridge Close.....10 G3
Brockhollands Road 23 B5
Brockworth Bypass 8 H3
Brockworth Road 4 H6/8 H4
Brome Road 7 D6
Bromley Road 20 F6
Brook House 31 C1
Brook Lane (Bream) 23 A4
Brook Lane (Glos.) 3 A1
Brook Street (Glos.) 16 G6
Brook Street (Mitcheldean) 40 F2
Brook Villas 26 F3
Brookfield Lane 4 H4

Brookfield Road (Churchdown)
.....................................4 H5
Brookfield Road (Glos.).......7 C4
Brookfield Villas....................6 H2
Brooklands Park 3 A4
Brooks Cottages 26 E3
Brookside.........................36 F5
Brookside Road.................33 D2
Brookside Villas...................6 H1
Brookthorpe Close.............11 D2
Broom Bungalows 6 G6
Broom Hill 17 A2
Broom House*, Baneberry Road
.....................................6 G6
Brummels Drive.................17 C3
Brunel Road.......................38 F2
Brunswest Court*, Parliament St.
.....................................16 F4
Brunswick Court*, Brunswick Sq.
.....................................16 F4
Brunswick Road.................16 F5
Brunswick Square 16 F4
Bruton Way 16 H3
Buchanan Avenue 17 C6
Buchanan Close 17 C6
Buckholt Road...................14 G6
Buckingham Drive 4 E2
Buckshaft Road.................35 A1
Buckstone Close...........18 F4/F5
Buddleia Close 13 D1
Bull Lane 16 F3
Bullfinch Road 7 A5
Bullfinch Way.....................3 B2
Bullring, The......................40 F2
Bulwark Avenue 38 G3
Bulwark Road 38 E2
Bungalows, The (Coalway) 20 E1
Bungalows, The (Lydney) ...27 C4
Bungalows, The*, Mt. Pleasant
.....................................28 E5
Burford Mews 6 G3
Burleigh Croft 7 D3
Burnet Close 12 G1
Burns Avenue 11 C1
Burnt Barn Road 38 G2
Burnt Houses....................20 E6
Burton Cottages 32 H2
Bury Bar Lane 36 G5
Buscombe Gardens.............8 F4
Bush Hay 4 F4
Butlers Mead 26 G3
Buttercup Lawn 13 B3
Buttermilk Lane 4 F3
Buttington 7 D6
Buttington Cottages 38 F5
Buttington Hill 38 E5
Buttington Road.................38 E4
Buttington Terrace 38 F5
Butts, The (Glos.) 12 G1
Butts, The (Newent) 36 G5
Byard Road 5 B6
Bybrook Gardens 11 D4
Bybrook Road 11 D4
Byford Close 39 C4
Byfords Road.....................39 C4
Byre, The...........................12 H1
Byron Avenue 11 C1

C

Cadbury Close......................8 F5
Caerleon Way 38 G3
Caerwent Lane 38 H3
Caesar Road 5 C6

Caesars Close...................27 C5
Caird Street 38 E2
Calderdale 7 D6
Caledonian Road 13 A3
Calendula Court...................4 E2
Calspick Way.......................3 B4
Calton Road.........................6 E6
Camberley Close..................8 E3
Cambourne Place 28 E4
Cambridge Street 16 H4
Camellia Walk 10 G3
Camomile Close 7 D6
Camomile Green 29 D6
Camp Road 38 F3
Campbell Close 3 C2
Campbell Road 18 F6
Campden Road 12 E3
Campion Close 12 G1
Cams Ground 9 B1
Canal Way 1 B5
Canning Road 3 C5
Cannons Court 14 E2
Cannop Road 24 E1
Capel Road 13 A3
Captains Green Road 24 G2
Cardinal Drive 11 A3
Carisbrook Road (Mitcheldean)
.....................................40 F1
Carisbrooke Road (Glos.) 8 E5
Carmarthen Street.............16 H6
Carne Place 7 A2
Carpenter Cottages............19 C6
Carters Orchard.................10 H3
Cartway Green 34 E3
Carwardine Field 7 C5
Casey Close 6 G2
Castle Cottages 7 D3
Castle Crescent 21 C4
Castle Gardens 37 C1
Castle View 37 C4
Castleford Gardens 37 B3
Castleford Hill................37 B2/B3
Castlemeads Court 16 E2
Castleton Road 7 B4
Cathedral Court*, London Road
.....................................6 G1
Catherine Court...................6 E4
Catkin Close 10 G6
Catshill.............................30 F1
Caudle Close 30 F1
Caudle Cottages 30 F2
Caudle Lane 30 F1
Causeway Road 34 F1
Causeway, The 10 F4
Cavendish Avenue 4 H4
Cavendish Building*,
       Eastgate Street 16 G3
Cavendish Buildings (Lydney)
.....................................27 D3
Cecil Road..........................5 C4
Cedar Close 38 G2
Cedar Road 8 H4
Cedar Way........................18 F5
Cedardean.........................34 E2
Cedars, The*, Hucclecote Rd.
.....................................8 F4
Cedarwood Drive...............12 E2
Celandine Court 38 G3
Cemetery Road 6 G5
Centenary Mews 4 E3
Central Avenue 40 G2
Central Road 6 E4
Centurion Close...................7 C5

Centurion Road 27 C4
Centurions Walk 19 D2
Chaceley Close (Abbeymead)
.....................................7 C6
Chaceley Close (Quedgeley)
.....................................10 G5
Chadbournes 4 F3
Chadwick Close..................11 D3
Chaffinch Close 3 A2
Chalford Road 12 E4
Chamwells Avenue 2 H5
Chamwells Walk 2 H5
Chancel Close 7 A3
Channel View 38 G2
Chantry Close 28 F3
Chapel Apartments 19 D1
Chapel Cottages 21 C1
Chapel Gardens 10 H6
Chapel Hay Close 4 G5
Chapel Hay Lane..................4 H5
Chapel Road (Berry Hill) 17 D4
Chapel Road (Viney Hill) 25 D3
Chapel Walk 18 G2
Charlecote Avenue 11 C5
Charles Street 16 H4
Charleswood Road 24 E3
Charlies Way 8 F3
Charlock Close 12 G1
Charlton Court*, Asylum La. 6 F1
Charlton Way........................3 A4
Charnwood Court 27 B4
Charter Court.....................16 H5
Chartist Piece 40 G5
Chartist Way (Chepstow) ...38 G2
Chartist Way (Staunton) 40 F5
Chartwell Close 5 A5
Chase Lane 6 H3
Chase, The (Churchdown) ..4 G5
Chase, The (Glos.) 7 B6
Chatcombe Road 16 H6
Chatsworth Avenue 11 C4/C5
Chaucer Close.....................5 D6
Chedworth House 10 H2
Chedworth Lane 12 E2
Chelsea Court 16 F3
Cheltenham Road......2 H6/3 A6
Cheltenham Road East 3 C4
Chepstow Road.................21 D1
Chequers Road 6 G4
Cherrington Drive 7 C6
Cherry Bank......................36 F6
Cherry Close 10 G6
Cherry Gardens 8 E3
Cherry Tree Close 8 E3
Cherry Tree Court*, Rectory Rd.
.....................................13 A1
Cherry Tree Lane...............18 F5
Cherry Walk.......................27 C3
Cherrywood Gardens 12 E2
Cherston Court 7 C3
Chervil Close 12 H1
Chesford Drive 4 G3
Cheshire Road 3 C3
Chesmann Court 2 F5
Chester Road 7 A3
Chesterton Court 2 F3
Chestnut Close (Hardwicke)
.....................................10 G6
Chestnut Close (Mile End).18 F5
Chestnut Cottages (Highnam)
.....................................9 B1
Chestnut Cottages (Maisemore)
.....................................1 A2

Chestnut Road 7 C6
Chestnuts, The 16 F5
Cheviot Close 10 G5
Cheyney Close 6 H5
Chickadee 21 B5
Chillingworth Mews 16 F4
Chiltern Road 10 G5
Chirch View 17 C3
Chislet Way 11 D4
Chivenor Way 11 A4
Choirs Close 7 C5
Chosen Drive 4 F4
Chosen View Cottages 8 E5
Chosen Way 7 D3
Church Cottages (Clearwell)
.....................................19 C6
Church Cottages (Glos.) ...12 E5
Church Drive (Glos.) ...10 H4/H5
Church Drive (Parkend)......23 D1
Church Gardens 28 E3
Church Hill........................29 C5
Church Lane (Glos.) 7 B3
Church Lane (Hardwicke) ..15 A2
Church Lane (Whaddon) 12 E5
Church Rise.........................1 A2
Church Road (Chepstow) ...37 D3
Church Road (Churchdown) 4 G5
Church Road (Cinderford) ..34 E5
Church Road (Clearwell)....21 C1
Church Road (Longlevens) ..3 A5
Church Road (Lydbrook).....29 C5
Church Road (Lydney) 28 E2
Church Road (Maisemore)
.....................................1 A2/A2
Church Road (Newnham)
.....................................35 B5/B6
Church Road (Soudley).....35 B4
Church Road Place 34 F3
Church Row.......................37 C1
Church Square 26 G2
Church Street (Glos.)........16 E5
Church Street (Littledean) ..34 H4
Church Street (Newent) 36 F5
Church Street (St. Briavels)
.....................................21 C4
Church View 29 C5
Church Walk (Broadwell)...18 F6
Church Walk (Littledean)...34 H3
Church Walk (Parkend).....23 D1
Church Walk (Viney Hill) ...25 C4
Church Way (Blakeney) 26 G2
Church Way (Glos.)............7 A5
Church Way (Newent)........36 G5
Churchdown Lane 8 F4
Churchfield Road...............13 C3
Churchill Road 5 D4/6 E4
Churchill Way....................40 F2
Churchview Drive 7 B3
Cider Mill Close*,
       Summer Ho. Lane 38 H3
Cinder Hill (Coleford).........19 D2
Cinder Hill (St. Briavels) ...21 B4
Cinderford Road 26 F1
Cinderhill Way 30 F1
Clapham Court 16 H2
Clare Street 16 E2
Claremont Court 6 F1
Claremont House*, London Rd.
.....................................16 H2
Claremont Road 16 H2
Clarence Street 16 G3
Clarence Walk*, Clarence Street
.....................................16 G3

Clarendon Close 38 H4
Claridge Close 13 B1
Clarkia Close 3 D2
Clarks Lane 26 E3
Claudians Close 7 C4
Claudius Way 27 C4
Clay Road 18 E2
Clayburn Close 9 B1
Clays Road 22 E1
Clearwater Drive 10 F4
Cleeve Mill Estate 36 H5
Cleeve Mill Lane 36 H4/H5
Cleeve Rise 36 G5
Cleeve Road 12 H1
Clegram Road 5 D4
Clement Cottages 6 G3
Clement Street 6 G3
Clements End Road 22 E1
Clevedon Road 6 F5
Cliff View 38 E4
Clifton Road 16 F6
Clomoney Way 3 B4
Close, The 18 F5
Clover Close 20 E4
Clover Drive 15 C1
Clover Piece 7 B5
Co-op Cottages 29 D6
Coalway Road 20 E1
Coberley Road..................12 E2
Cochran Close 4 G4
Cockshoot Hill 21 B5
Colchester Close (Mitcheldean)
....40 F3
Colchester Close (Westbury)
....32 G5
Coldharbour Lane 36 E1
Coldharbour Road 21 A6
Coldray Close 6 H2
Cole Avenue 11 B2
Colebridge Avenue 3 A6
Coleford Road (Bream) 22 G5
Coleford Road (Tutshill)......37 B3
Colerne Drive 8 F4
Colin Road 7 B2
Collafield 34 H1
College Court 16 F3
College Fields 3 B5
College Green 16 F3
College Road....................34 E2
College Street 16 F3
Colliers Court 34 G2
Colliers Field 34 E2
Collingbourne Road 6 G4
Collingwood Close 38 G4
Collins Close 40 F5
Colsty Meadow 26 F3
Coltishall Close 11 A5
Coltman Close 6 H2
Columbia Close 16 H2
Colwell Avenue 8 E2
Colwellschool Close 6 G2
Combrook Close 13 C1
Commerce Road 4 G1
Commercial Road 16 E3
Commercial Street 34 F3
Compton Close (Glos.) 4 E1
Compton Close (Staunton) 40 F5
Concorde Way.....................6 H4
Conduit Street 16 H6
Coney Hill Parade 7 A4
Coney Hill Road 6 H4/7 B4
Conifers, The......................6 G4
Coniston Road....................3 A5

Connemara Close 36 F6
Constitution Walk*,
    Eastgate Precinct 16 G3
Conway Court 17 D3
Conway Road 8 E3
Cooks Orchard.....................2 F6
Cookson Terrace...............28 G3
Coomb Drive 34 E6
Coombe Park Estate 19 D1
Coombs Road 17 C6
Coombs, The.....................17 C6
Coopers Court.....................8 H6
Coopers End 10 H3
Coopers Road 17 C2
Coopers View 8 H6
Coopers Way 36 G5
Copley Drive 19 D2
Copper Beech Grove 10 G4
Copperfield Close 12 H1
Coppice Daw Pitch 39 C6
Coppice Mews.....................8 E4
Coppice Road 29 B3
Copse, The 7 C4
Coral Close 11 B2
Cordingley Close 4 G4/G5
Coriander Drive 3 D3
Corinium Avenue 7 B1
Corncroft Lane 13 A3
Corner Road 24 E4
Cornfield Drive (Glos.)........10 G6
Cornfield Drive (Hardwicke)
....15 C1
Cornflower Road 7 B6
Cornish Houses.................35 A1
Corolin Road 11 B2
Coronation Cottages 35 B6
Coronation Grove 6 H1
Coronation Road 34 F4
Cotswold Gardens 3 B4
Cotswold View 5 B5
Cottage Field 9 B1
Cottages, The 34 H4
Cotteswold Road 6 G5
Cotton Close 7 D6
Council Houses, The 32 H6
Council Villas (Clearwell) ...19 B6
Council Villas (Edge End) ...18 G2
Council Villas (Sling) 20 E6
County Crescent 6 G2
Court Cottages 2 H1
Court End 14 E4
Court Farm Lane 40 F2
Court Gardens (Glos.) 5 B5
Court Gardens (Westbury) 32 G6
Court Lane 36 F5
Court Place 7 B5
Court Road (Glos.)........8 H5/H6
Court Road (Lydney) 27 A4
Court Road (Newent) 36 G4
Courtfield Cottages 40 F2
Courtfield Road 10 G5
Courtyard, The*, London Road
....16 H2
Cousley Close 8 E4
Coverham Close 17 D3
Coverham Road 17 C4
Cowley Road 12 E2
Coxmore Close 8 E4
Coxs Way (Bream) 23 B4
Coxs Way (Glos.) 8 E5
Crabtree Road...................33 D2
Craddock Road 36 F5
Cranham Close 13 C1

Cranham Lane.....................4 H6
Cranwell Close 13 A1
Craven Drive 4 E3
Crawshay Place.................34 E3
Crease, The 36 G5
Credon Road 7 C2
Crescent Close 17 C6
Crescent, The (Berry Hill) ..17 C4
Crescent, The (Brockworth) 8 H5
Crescent, The (Coleford).....19 D1
Crescent, The (Glos.) 6 G1
Crescent, The (Mitcheldean)
....40 F1
Crescent, The (Sunnybank)
....17 C6
Crescentdale 2 G3/H3
Crest Way 7 D2
Criftycraft Lane 4 G6
Crispin Close 3 A4
Crock Mead 7 C5
Croft Close (Glos.)...............4 H5
Croft Close (Newent).........36 H4
Croft Road........................36 G4
Crofts, The 36 G4
Cromwell Lane 19 C6
Cromwell Road 38 G2
Cromwell Street.................16 G4
Crooked End Place 30 H1
Crosby Close 8 F5
Cross Bank House*, High Street
....28 E3
Cross Keys 21 D4
Cross Keys Lane 16 F3
Cross, The (Drybrook).......31 D2
Cross, The*, High Street ...19 C6
Crow Ash 17 C4
Crow Ash Road 17 C4
Crowfield Lane 39 D2
Crown Close 39 B2
Crown Cottages (Parkend) 23 D1
Crown Cottages (Stowe Grn.)
....21 B3
Crown Lane (Parkend) 23 C1
Crown Lane (St. Briavels) ..21 C4
Crown Lane (Yorkley) 24 G3
Crown Meadow 20 F2
Crucible Close 19 D2
Crucible Court 19 D2
Crump Place 28 E5
Crypt Court 11 C2
Crypt, The 39 B2
Cullimore View 34 E6
Cullingham Close..............40 F5
Cullis Lane 18 F5
Culver Street 36 F6
Cupola Close 19 D2
Curlew Road 7 A5
Curtis Hayward Drive 10 G4
Cut and Fry Road 25 A3
Cypress Gardens................3 B4

D

Daffodil Close 7 C6
Dainty Street 16 H6
Dale Close 6 F6
Damson Close 13 C1
Danby Close (Cinderford) ..34 G3
Danby Close (Yorkley).......25 A2
Danby Road......................25 A2
Dancers Hill 7 C5
Dancey Road......................3 D3
Dane Close (Glos.) 3 A4
Danes Close (Chepstow) ...37 D1

Danes Hill 38 E4
Daniels Meadow 11 A3
Danwood Court 5 D4
Darell Close 10 H6
Darleydale Close 10 F5
Darren Road 17 D4
Dart Close 10 H3
Darters Close....................28 E3
Darwin Road 6 G6
Daventry Terrace...............16 H6
Davey Close 15 D1
Davillian Court 11 A2
Davis Court 37 C2
Dawes, The 10 H5
Dean Court 27 B4
Dean Crescent 34 H4
Dean Meadows 40 G3
Dean Place 34 H3
Dean Road 35 A5
Dean View 34 E6
Deanpool Court 21 D1
Deans Gardens 37 D1
Deans Hill 37 D1
Deans Row 2 E5
Deans Terrace 2 E6
Deans Walk (Drybrook) 31 D2
Deans Walk (Glos.) 16 G1
Deans Way 16 G1
Deansway Road 40 F1
Deer Park 24 H2
Deer Park Road...................8 E2
Deerhurst Close 13 C1
Deerhurst Place 10 G4
Dell View 37 D2
Dell, The 7 C3
Delta Way 8 G5/G6
Denbigh Drive 38 H3/H4
Denecroft 34 E2
Denehurst 30 H4
Denham Close...................11 C4
Denmark Court*, Denmark Road
....2 G6
Denmark Drive...................38 E5
Denmark Road.....................2 E5
Denton Place 21 C4
Derby Court 6 G2
Derby Road 6 G3
Desford Close 7 D6
Devonia Cottages 31 B2
Dianas Close 7 D5
Dickens Close 6 F6
Dickens Mews 6 F6
Didbrook Mews 13 C1
Dimore Close 10 F6/G6
Dinely Street 16 H5
Dingles Meadow 7 B6
Dinglewell 7 D4
Discovery Road 7 D5
Dockham Road 34 F2/G3
Dockins Hill 32 G2
Dockins Hill Way 32 G2
Dodington Close 7 B4
Dombey Bungalows 11 C1
Domby Close.....................19 D2
Dora Walk 6 F4
Dorney Road 5 D5
Dorrit Close 6 F5
Double View.......................34 F4
Dovedale Close 10 F5
Doverdale Drive 3 B5
Dowding Way 4 G4
Dowles Cottages 39 C2
Down Hatherley Lane 4 F1

Downy Close 10 G3
Drake Close..........................3 D2
Drayton Close 13 A1
Drayton Way 7 A6
Drews Close 4 G5
Drews Court 4 G5
Driffield Road 27 A5
Drivemoor 13 B2
Druids Lane 7 A4
Druids Oak 10 G5
Dry Meadow Lane 3 A2
Drybrook Road 31 C3
Dryland Mews 8 F5
Ducie Street 6 F4
Duke of Beaufort Court 5 D6
Dukeries, The*, Westgate Street
....16 E2
Duncroft Road 7 D2
Dunlin Close 10 F4
Dunstan Glen 4 H5
Dunster Close 11 B4
Dunstone Place*, Stars Pitch
....40 F2
Durand Close..........................3 A3
Durham Road 7 A3
Duttons Lane 30 H3
Dynevor Street.......................6 F4

E

Eagle Way 7 A6
Eardisland Road 12 E3
East Cottages 19 C6
East Link 40 G1
East Street 21 C4
East View 35 A5
Eastbach Court 29 A6
Eastbrook Road......................7 A3
Eastcott Way 4 E3
Eastern Avenue (Glos.) ..6 G5/H4
Eastern Avenue (Mitcheldean)
....40 F3
Eastern Way 35 A1
Eastfield Mews 6 F6
Eastgate House*, Eastgate St.
....16 G3
Eastgate Shopping Precinct
....16 G3
Eastgate Street 16 G3/G4
Eastville Caravan Park 17 C2
Eastville Close.......................6 H3
Eastwood Road...................31 D3
Ebor Road 7 A2
Ebrington Close 7 B3
Eddys Lane 30 F4
Edenwall 20 F3
Edenwall Road 20 E4
Edge End Road 18 F5
Edge Hills Close 34 F2
Edge Hills Road 34 F2
Edgehill 32 G2
Edgeworth Close 7 C6
Edinburgh Place 20 F1
Edison Close 11 A6
Edith Cottages.....................15 D1
Edmond Road 37 D5
Edward Massey Gardens*,
    Matson Avenue 13 A2
Edwards Close 29 C4
Edwy Parade 2 E6
Elderberry Mews 3 D3
Eldersfield Close 10 G3
Elderwood Way 11 C2
Eliot Close 11 C1

Ellesmere Close 7 D3
Ellison Close 8 E5
Ellwood Road 20 E4
Elm Close (Glos.)...................4 F3
Elm Close (Tutshill) 37 B4
Elm Drive 8 H5
Elm Grove 39 C4
Elm Road 37 B3
Elm Villas 3 B2
Elmbridge Home 7 A1
Elmbridge Road.....................7 A1
Elmbridge Villas...................39 D1
Elmdale 37 C2
Elmdean 34 E1/E2
Elmgrove Estate 10 G6
Elmgrove Road 8 E5
Elmgrove Road East 10 G6
Elmgrove Road West...........10 F6
Elming House*, Southgate St.
....16 E5
Elmira Road 12 F1
Elmleaze 3 B5/B6
Elmore Lane East 10 H2
Elmore Lane West 10 E3
Elms, The 37 D5
Emerald Close 11 C2
Empire Way 5 B6
Enborne Close......................11 D4
Ennerdale Avenue 3 A4
Epney Road..........................11 C2
Ermin Park 8 H4/H5
Ermin Street 8 H5
Ermine Parade 8 H5
Erminster Drive 8 E4
Essex Close 4 E1
Estate Road..........................33 D1
Estcourt Close 2 G5
Estcourt Road 2 F5
Etheridge Place 6 G2
Evenlode Road 11 D4
Evergreen Walk 3 B4
Exmouth Place 37 D2

F

Fair View 38 F1
Fair View Caravan Park 1 C6
Fairfield Close 19 D2
Fairfield Court*, Rectory Road
....13 A1
Fairfield Road (Chepstow) ..38 F2
Fairfield Road (Lydney) 27 D3
Fairfields 34 E3
Fairford Way 6 H4
Fairhaven Avenue 8 H5
Fairmile Gardens 2 F4
Fairmoor Close 23 D1
Fairplay Cottages................32 F3
Fairwater Park 7 B2
Fairways Avenue..................19 D2
Fairways Drive.......................3 D1
Falcon Close 3 A3
Faldo Close 7 D6
Falfield Road 11 C2
Falkner Street 16 H5
Fancy Hill 24 F2
Fancy Road 24 E2
Far Sandfield..........................4 G4
Faraday Close 6 F4
Farm Cottages 7 C2
Farm Flats 36 G5
Farm Mews 16 G6
Farm Road 30 H3
Farm Street 16 G6

Farmington Close*, Kingscote Dr.
....7 C6
Farrant Avenue 4 E3
Farriers Court 17 D6
Farriers End.........................10 H3
Farthing Croft.........................9 A2
Fennel Close 13 A1
Fern Court 38 G3
Fern Lawn 13 B3
Fern Road 20 F6
Ferndale Close (Cinderford)
....34 F2
Ferndale Close (Glos.) 2 H3
Fernyfield..............................32 H1
Ferry Gardens 10 F4
Ferry Way 38 H5
Fetter Hill 20 F5
Field Buildings 11 D6
Field Court Drive 10 G5
Field Court Gardens 10 G5/H5
Field End 4 E2
Field House 11 D5
Fieldcote Drive 7 D4
Fielden 13 B2
Fieldfare 7 B6
Filbert Close 13 B1
Filton Way 6 H4
Finch Road 3 B3
Finchmoor Mews 2 F4
Finlay Place 6 F6
Finlay Road 6 F6/12 E1
Fir Tree Cottages................23 B4
Fir View Road 35 A1
Fircroft Close 7 D3
Fircroft Road 2 F3
Firethorne Close 2 H3
Firs, The 2 F6
Firwood Drive 12 E2
Fishermans Walk 38 G3
Fitzosborn Close 38 E1
Flats, The 38 E4
Flaxley House 6 G1
Flaxley Road 11 D2
Flaxley Street.......................34 F3
Fleming Close 3 A3
Flower Way 2 H5
Folders, The 27 D4
Foley Close 11 D2
Foley Road 36 F6
Folland Avenue 8 F5
Folly, The 23 B1
Forbes Close 7 D5
Ford House Road 36 H2
Forest Parade 27 D3
Forest Patch 17 C3
Forest Rise (Cinderford) 34 G2
Forest Rise (Lydbrook) 29 C5
Forest Road (Bream)..........23 B4
Forest Road (Cinderford)....34 F3
Forest Road (Lydney) 27 D3
Forest Road (Mile End) 18 F4
Forest Road (Milkwall)......20 E4
Forest Road (Rua. Woodside)
....30 H3
Forest Vale Road 31 D6
Forest View (Cinderford) 34 E6
Forest View (Drybrook) 31 D2
Forest View*, New Road 29 C6
Forest View Park 34 E3
Forest View Road 12 E3
Forge Hill 29 B3
Forge Row 29 B3
Forsdene Walk.....................20 F1

Forsyte Way 6 H4
Forsythia Close 4 E2
Fosse Close 7 C5
Foundry Houses 20 F1
Foundry Road 34 E2
Fountain Square 16 F2
Fountain Way 38 H3
Fox Close 7 D6
Fox Elms Road 12 E3
Fox Run 11 A3
Foxcote 2 H4
Foxes Bridge Road 33 D2
Foxglove Close 7 C6
Foxglove Way 20 E4
Foxleigh Crescent 3 C4
Foxs Lane 20 F1
Foxtail Close 6 G6
Foxwell Drive 7 D3
Frampton Road 5 D4
Freemans Orchard...............36 F5
Freeminers Way 34 F2
Fretherne Road 11 D2
Friars Walk...........................36 F4
Friary Road 7 C5
Frobisher Mews....................3 D1
Frog Furlong Lane.................3 C1
Frog Lane 39 C4
Frogmore Road 39 C4
Fullers Court*, Westgate Street
....16 E2
Furlong Road 6 E4
Furnace Close 34 E3
Furnace Cottages (Newent)
....36 F3
Furnace Cottages (Parkend)
....23 D1
Furnace Lane.......................36 F4
Furnace Valley 26 E3
Furze Croft 10 H6
Furze, The 12 G1

G

Gaggs Row 30 G3
Gainsborough Drive 11 C3
Gallops, The 5 B5
Gambier Parry Gardens........2 F5
Garage Flats 28 E1
Garden City Way 38 E2
Garden Villas 2 F4
Garden Way 2 H5
Gardeners Way 36 F5
Gardiners Close.....................4 E3
Garlandstone Walk 5 C5
Garnalls Road 13 A1/A2
Garvey Close........................38 H3
Gasworks Cottages...............6 G2
Gascoignes Villas 11 B1
Gatmeres Road 13 A2
Gatton Way 7 D2
Gazelle Close 10 H3
Gentian House 15 C1
George Lane 34 H3
George Place 17 D4
George Road 24 H2
George Street 16 H3
George Whitefield Close 13 A1
Georgian Close 13 C2
Gerald Close 11 D3
Gibraltar Way 38 H5
Gibson Road 3 C2
Gifford Close 3 A4
Gilbert Road 3 A4
Gilberts Lane 12 F6

Giles Cox............................10 H5
Gilpin Avenue 7 D2
Gimson Close 11 D3
Gladstone Road 5 C5
Glebe Close (Mitcheldean) 40 F1
Glebe Close (Newent) 36 F4
Glebe Court 36 F4
Glebe Road 36 E5
Glebe Way.........................36 F4
Glencairn Avenue 11 C4
Glencarn Place 17 D4
Glencoe Lane 32 G2
Glendower Close................3 D1
Glenmore Road*,
    Forest View Park 34 E4
Glenville Parade*,
    Hucclecote Road 8 E4
Glevum Close 2 H5
Glevum Shopping Centre ..13 B1
Glevum Way 13 C1
Gloucester North Bypass
    ....1 C5/3 A3
Gloucester Road (Coleford)
    ....19 D1
Gloucester Road (Mitcheldean)
    ....40 G3
Gloucester Road (Staunton)
    ....40 G4
Gloucester Road (Tutshill)..37 B3
Gloucester South Bypass ..10 H6
Gloucester South West Bypass
    ....5 A6/11 A1
Gloucester Street 36 G5
Glover Close 35 A2
Glynbridge Court 6 F4
Goddard Way 11 D3
Golden Close.....................11 C3
Golden Vale 4 F3
Golden Valley Bypass 3 D4
Goldsborough Road 6 H4
Golf Club Lane 8 G6/14 G1
Goode Court 27 D3
Goodmoor Crescent 4 E3
Goodridge Avenue.............11 A1
Goodwin Court.....................6 E4
Goodyere Street 16 H5
Gooses Neck Lane 29 C3
Gordon Close 9 B1
Gorse Bungalows 17 C5
Gorse Close 13 D1
Gorse Lane 20 E6
Gorsty Knoll 20 F4
Goshawk Road 10 H2
Goss Wood Corner 10 G5
Gothic Cottages 6 F2
Gouda Way 16 F2
Graces Pitch 36 G5
Grafton Road........................2 H6
Graham Gardens.................2 H6
Grahamstown Grove 37 D4
Grahamstown Road 37 D4
Grange Court Lane 39 C5
Grange Road......................11 C2
Grange, The (Glos.) 6 H1
Grange, The*, Holmwood Drive
    ....11 D3
Granley Court*, Gladstone Road
    ....5 C5
Gransmoor Grange 8 F4
Granville Street 5 C5
Granville Terrace................37 C3
Grasby Close.......................7 C4
Grasmere Road...................3 A5

Grasmere Way 38 H4
Gray Close............................3 B2
Grayling Close......................7 C6
Great Grove..........................7 B4
Great Western Court*,
    Millbrook Street 6 F3
Great Western Road 16 H3
Grebe Close 7 B6
Green Acre (Bream) 23 B6
Green Acre (Glos.) 8 H6
Green Bank 14 H1
Green Bottom 34 H1
Green Close (Brockworth)....8 H6
Green Close (Green Street)
    ....14 H2
Green Gardens 14 H1
Green Hedges 37 A4
Green Lane (Churchdown) ..4 G5
Green Lane (Glos.) 8 E5
Green Lane (Hardwicke) 15 B1
Green Park 15 C1
Green Pippin Close 7 A1
Green Street (Brockworth)
    ....14 H2/H3
Green Street (Chepstow)....38 E2
Green Street Cottages 15 D4
Green Way 8 H6
Green, The (Glos.)................8 E5
Green, The (Newnham) 35 A6
Green, The*, Green La..........4 G5
Greenaways.......................36 F4
Greenbank Close 31 D3
Greenfield Close 29 C4
Greenfield Road (Coleford) 17 D6
Greenfield Road (Lydbrook)
    ....29 C4
Greenfields 4 E1
Greenhill Close 34 G2
Greenhill Court 11 B3
Greenhill Drive 11 A2
Greenway 34 H2
Greenway Road..................34 E4
Greenways 28 E2
Greenways Drive 20 E3
Greenwood Close 8 F5
Grenadier Close 7 D5
Grenville Close 3 D1
Greville Close 2 E5
Greyfriars 16 F3
Greyhound Gardens 3 B4
Grierson Close 8 F5
Griffon Close 10 H2
Grisedale Close....................3 A4
Grosvenor House*, Station Rd.
    ....16 G3
Grosvenor Road 6 H1
Grove Crescent (Coleford) 17 D6
Grove Crescent (Glos.) 7 A2
Grove End Cottages 9 C5
Grove End Villas 9 D6
Grove Lane 24 H6
Grove Park 24 E4
Grove Road (Berry Hill) 17 C3
Grove Road (Glos.) 3 D4
Grove Road (Lydney) 27 C2
Grove Road (Whitecroft) 24 E4
Grove Street 6 F3
Grovelands 7 C3
Guild House*, Denmark Rd. 2 F6
Guinea Street 16 H1
Guise Close 10 H5
Gurney Avenue 11 D3/D4
Gwentlands Close 38 E2

Gwentlands Flats...............38 E2
Gwy Court 37 C3

H

Hadfield Close 40 F5
Hadow Way 10 H5
Hadrian Close 27 C4
Hadrians Way 7 C4
Hailes Road 7 B4
Halford House 11 C1
Halton Way 11 A5
Hamer Street........................6 G2
Hamlen Close 39 C4
Hammond Court 7 B2
Hammond Way 7 B2
Hampden Way 16 G4
Hampshire Gardens 19 C2
Hampton Mews*, Hams Road
    ....27 D4
Hampton Place 4 E1
Hampton Street 8 F4
Hams Road 27 D4
Hang Hill Road 23 A4
Hangerberry......................29 B4
Hangerberry New Road 30 G5
Hanman Road 6 F4
Hannah Place 3 C2
Hanover Close (Chepstow) 37 C1
Hanover Close (Glos.)..........3 D2
Hanover Court (Cinderford) 34 E2
Hanover Court (Sedbury) 3 D4
Hanover Way 4 E2
Harbour Road.........28 F3/G4/H6
Harbury Mews 6 G3
Hardwick 37 D2
Hardwick Avenue...............38 E2
Hardwick Green..................15 C1
Hardwick Hill 38 E2
Hardwick Hill Lane.............38 E2
Hardwick Terrace 37 D2
Hardwicke Court 15 A3
Hare Lane 16 G2/G3
Harebell Place 7 C6
Harescombe Drive 6 G2
Haresfield Lane 15 C2
Haresfield Lodge*, Norbury Av.
    ....12 H1
Harewood Close 11 C4
Harleys Field 7 B4
Harness Close 5 B5
Harold Road 25 A2
Harptree Way*, Glebe Cl. ..40 F1
Harris Close 4 G4
Harrison Close....................35 A6
Harrison Way 28 E5
Hart Green.........................34 E5
Hart Lane 30 G1
Hartington Road 5 C5
Hartland Road 6 F5
Harvest Way 10 H6
Harvey Close........................5 C6
Harveys Lane 24 H2
Harwell Close 11 D4
Hasfield Close 10 G4
Hastings Road 34 E3
Hatfield Road 6 G4
Hathaway Close 11 B1
Hatherley Road 6 F5
Hathorn Road 4 F6
Hatton Close 30 G5
Havelock Road 8 E3
Haven Court 3 A6
Haw Road 18 G2

Hawk Close 7 B6
Hawker Hill........................40 F3
Hawkwell Cottages 31 C4
Haworth Close....................10 H3
Hawthorn Close.................38 G2
Hawthorn Court 27 D4
Hawthorn Drive (Glos.) 4 E3
Hawthorn Drive (Sling) 22 E1
Hawthorne Avenue 7 A6
Hawthorns Road 31 C1
Hawthorns, The (Bream) ...23 B4
Hawthorns, The (Lydney) ..27 D4
Haycroft Drive 13 B2
Haydale Gardens 3 A4
Hayes Court*, Fircroft Rd. ...2 F3
Hayward Close 7 B4
Hazel Close 2 H4
Hazel Court 7 B2
Hazel Field 31 D1
Hazel Road 31 D1
Hazel Villas 31 D1
Hazelcroft.............................4 F3
Hazeldean 34 E2
Hazels, The 7 C4
Hazelton Close 6 F5
Headlam Close 11 D4
Headland, The....................38 H4
Healey Mews*, London Rd...6 G1
Heasley Cottages 31 C1
Heathdean Road 3 D3
Heather Avenue 13 D1
Heather Close 38 G3
Heathville Road 6 F1
Hedgerow, The 2 H5
Hembury Close 10 F6
Hemmingsdale Road...........5 C2
Hempsted Lane 5 B5/C3
Hendingham Close 11 B3
Hendrick Drive....................37 D4
Henley Place 5 D6
Henley Road 23 B4
Henry Road 6 F1
Henry Ryder Close 7 D5
Henry Street 16 H2
Herbert Howells Close.......28 E3
Herbert Street 6 G3
Herberts Way 25 A4
Heron Way...........................7 A6
Hethersett Road 6 G3
Hewelsfield Lane 21 C5
Hewlett Way 35 A1
Heywood Road 34 F2
Hickley Gardens 8 H5
High Beech Lane 38 F1
High Beech Road................18 F4
High Delf Court 20 E1
High Delf Way 24 E4
High Meadow......................13 B1
High Nash 19 D2
High Orchard Street...........16 E5
High Road 40 G2
High Row 29 B3
High Street (Aylburton) 28 F1
High Street (Blakeney).......26 F3
High Street (Bream)...........23 A5
High Street (Chepstow) 37 D2
High Street (Cinderford) 34 E1
High Street (Clearwell) 19 C6
High Street (Coleford) 19 D1
High Street (Drybrook) 31 D1
High Street (Glos.)...............6 F4
High Street (Huntley) 39 B5
High Street (Littledean) 34 H3

High Street (Lydney) **28** E2
High Street (Mitcheldean) ..**40** F2
High Street (Newent) **36** F4
High Street (Newnham) **35** B6
High Street (Ruardean) **30** F1
High Street (St. Briavels)....**21** C4
High Street (The Pludds) **30** F4
High Street (Upton St. Leo.)
................................**13** C3
High Street (Westbury) **32** G5
High View (Chepstow)........**37** D2
High View (Glos.).................**5** A5
Highbank Park **2** F4
Highbeech Road (Bream) ..**23** A5
Highbeech Road (Lydbrook)
................................**30** E4
Highbury Estate.................**23** A5
Highbury Road....................**23** A5
Highclere Road **10** G3
Highfield...............................**26** F3
Highfield Close **23** A4
Highfield Lane **27** B5
Highfield Place (Coalway) ..**20** F1
Highfield Place (Glos.)........**6** H4
Highfield Rise **27** D4
Highfield Road (Bream) **23** A4
Highfield Road (Glos.).........**6** H4
Highfield Road (Lydney) **27** D4
Highfield Road (Rua. Woodside)
................................**30** G1
Highfield Villas..................**35** A5
Highgrove Way **3** D2
Highliffe Drive **11** A4
Highview Road (Cinderford)
................................**34** G3
Highview Road (Rua. Hill)
................................**31** A3/C3
Highview Road (Rua. Woodside)
................................**30** H3
Highview Road (Yorkley) ...**24** H2
Highview Way **23** B5
Highworth Road...................**6** F5
Hildyard Close...................**10** G6
Hill Cottages **2** F6
Hill Crest **9** B1
Hill Hay Road.....................**13** A2
Hill Road **12** E1
Hill Street............................**27** D3
Hill Top Lane **36** H3
Hill View **27** D3
Hill View Cottages **12** E3
Hillborough Road...............**12** E2
Hillcot Close **10** G4
Hillcrest Lane **18** F6
Hillcrest Road **17** C4
Hillersland Lane.................**17** B1
Hillfield Court.......................**6** G1
Hillfield Court Road **6** G1
Hillrise **23** B4
Hills Road **34** F2
Hillside Bungalows **23** B5
Hillside Close **23** B4
Hillside Estate....................**23** B4
Hillside Road (Drybrook) **31** C1
Hillside Road (Mitcheldean)
................................**40** G2
Hillside Terrace **29** C3
Hilltop (Bream)...................**23** A5
Hilltop (Chepstow) **38** E1
Hillview Avenue **8** H5
Hillview Drive **7** D3
Hillview House*, Larkhay Road
................................**8** E3
Hillview Rise **17** C3
Hillview Road **7** D3/8 E3
Hilton Close **5** B5
Hinton Road..........................**2** F5
Hitchen Hollow **38** H5
Hitchings **26** F3
Hocker Hill Street **37** D2
Hodges Way **34** E4
Holbrook **29** C6
Holbrook Villas...................**29** C6
Holcot Close **20** F1
Holcot Road **20** F2
Holland Court........................**2** G6
Hollins Close **37** D3
Hollow, The **31** B2
Holloway House **16** G2
Holly Close **38** G2
Holly Cottages **31** B2
Holly End **10** H5
Holly Grove, The **10** H6
Holly Lane **20** G6
Holly Tree Place **25** B4
Hollydean...........................**34** E1
Hollyhill Road **33** D2
Hollywell Road....................**40** F1
Holmleigh Parade **11** C3
Holmleigh Road..................**11** C2
Holmwood Close **11** D3
Holmwood Drive **11** C3/D3
Holst Way **11** D3
Holt, The **7** C4
Holtham Avenue **4** F2
Holts Road **36** F5
Holts Terrace **36** F4
Home Ground **7** C6
Homeleigh Court*, High St. ..**6** F4
Homestead Court*, Upton Lane
................................**7** D6
Honeysuckle Drive **7** C6
Honeythorn Close **5** B4
Honyatt Road........................**2** F6
Hooper Close **6** H5
Hop Garden, The*,
     Summer Ho. Lane **38** H3
Hope Cottages....................**24** E3
Hopes Close **28** E5
Hopewell **34** G2
Hopewell Close **38** H4
Hopewell Street **6** F3
Hopyard Lane **36** G3
Hornbeam Mews **2** H4
Horsbere Road **8** E3
Horsefair Lane **36** E4
Horselea **29** C4
Horsepool Lane **21** B6
Horsepool, The **17** C3
Horseshoe Cottages **39** C5
Horseshoe Drive **1** A5
Horseshoe Way **5** B5
Horsley Close **7** C6
Horton Road **6** G2
Horwell Hill **22** H4
Howard Place **8** E4
Howard Road **18** F6
Howard Street **16** G6/H6
Howcroft **4** G5
Howells Row **37** D3
Howgate Close **7** D6
Hucclecote Centre, The **8** F4
Hucclecote Court..................**7** D3
Hucclecote Lane **4** H6/8 H1
Hucclecote Lodge **8** F5
Hucclecote Mews **7** D4

Hucclecote Road..........**7** D3/8 F4
Hudson Lane **34** E6
Hudsons View **34** E6
Hughes Crescent **38** E2
Hughes Terrace..................**24** E2
Hunters Gate **13** B1
Huntfield Cottages **37** D2
Huntfield Road....................**37** D1
Huntley Close **7** C6
Huntley Court.....................**39** B5
Hunts Grove View **11** B6
Hurcombe Way **8** H5
Hurricane Road **8** G6/14 G1
Hurst Close **3** B4
Huxley Road **6** F4
Hyde Bank **35** A5
Hyde Close **6** G1
Hyde Lane (Glos.) **6** G1
Hyde Lane (Newnham) **35** A5
Hyde Park Corner **35** C4
Hyde View **19** B6
Hyett House*, Westgate Street
................................**16** F2

I

Ibis Walk **10** F4
Ida Villas **1** D3
Ince Castle Way **6** G3
India Road............................**6** G3
Inner Loop Road **38** F5
Innsworth Lane ...**3** A2/A4/B2/D2
Insley Gardens..............**7** C3/D2
Ironstone Close **23** A5
Itton Road **37** C1
Ivanhoe House **11** C1
Ivory Close **11** C3
Ivy Cottages **37** C5
Ivy Mews **6** F6

J

Jackson Crescent **3** C3
James Avenue **10** F4
James Close **10** F4
James Court **25** A3
James Drive **10** F4
James Grieve Road..............**7** D5
James Place **10** F5
James Row **10** F4
James Walk (Glos.) **10** F4
James Walk (Pillowell) **24** F4
James Way (Glos.) **10** F5
James Way (Hucclecote) **8** G5
Japonica Close **4** E2
Jasmine Close **13** B1
Jaynes Cottages **31** B3
Jaythorpe **13** B2
Jenner Close **7** D3
Jennings Walk **16** G4
Jersey Road..........................**6** F3
Jewson Close **11** D3
John Daniels Way **4** F5
John Woods Alley **16** H1
Johnsons Way **25** A2
Johnstone Close **40** F5
Johnstone Road..................**36** F5
Jordan Hill **32** G5
Jordans Way **2** F4
Jovial Collier Cottages, The
................................**30** H3
Jovial Colliers **30** H3
Joyford Hill **17** D3
Joys Green Road **29** C4
Jubilee Cottages **23** B5

Jubilee Lane **23** B5
Jubilee Place **40** F5
Jubilee Road (Lydney) **27** D5
Jubilee Road (Mitcheldean)
................................**32** G1
Judges Lodgings **32** G1
Julian Close **7** B3
Julius Way **27** C4
Juniper Avenue **12** H1
Juno Drive **27** B4
Jupiter Way **7** D5

K

Kaskelot Way **5** C5
Katherine Close **3** D1
Kaybourne Crescent **4** H4
Keats Avenue **11** C1
Keelings, The **34** E2
Kells Meend.........................**17** C3
Kemble Close **11** D3
Kemble Road.......................**11** D3
Kencourt Close **6** H1
Kendal Road **3** A6
Kendall Square **37** D3
Kenilworth Avenue **6** H1
Kenley House*, Rowandean
................................**34** F2
Kennedy Close **7** D2
Kennel Lane **14** H1
Kennett Gardens **13** C1
Kensley Vale **34** E4
Kent Close............................**4** H5
Kenton Drive **3** A4
Keriston Avenue **4** E4
Kerria Court **4** E2
Kestrel Gardens **10** H2
Kestrel Parade **3** B3
Keswick Close **2** H6
Kevin Close **7** B3
Kew Place **3** A4
Kibbles Lane **34** E6
Kidnalls Road......................**24** F4
Kilminster Court **4** E2
Kimberland Way **7** C5
Kimberley Close (Glos.)........**3** B5
Kimberley Close (Lydney) ..**27** D4
Kimberley Drive **27** D4
Kimbrose Way **16** F2
Kimbrose*, Southgate St. ...**5** D2
King Alfreds Road **38** E4
King Edwards Avenue **6** E5
Kingfisher Rise...................**10** F4
Kings Barton Street **16** H4
Kings Mead (Coleford) **19** D1
Kings Mead (Newnham) **35** A6
Kings Square.......................**16** G3
Kings Walk **16** G3
Kingscote Close **4** H5
Kingscote Drive **7** C6
Kingscroft Road **7** D4
Kingsholm Close **2** E5
Kingsholm Court **2** E5
Kingsholm Road **16** G1
Kingsholm Square **2** E5
Kingsley Road **6** G6
Kingsmark Lane **37** C1
Kingsmead **13** C1
Kingstone Avenue **7** D2
Kingsway **18** F6
Kingsway Lane **30** G2
Kinmoor **13** B2
Kipling Close **11** C1
Kitchener Avenue **6** E6

Klondyke Avenue 27 D4
Knights Crescent 36 E5
Knights Hill Road................30 G4
Knights Way 36 E5
Knockley Cottages.............23 B3
Knockley Patch 23 B3
Knoll Cottages 14 E5
Knoll, The*, Stroud Road ...16 F6
Knollys End 10 H5
Knowles Road 6 F4
Knox Road.........................23 D6

L

Laburnum Gardens 10 H4
Laburnum Road 11 D1
Laburnum Way 38 G2
Lacca Close*, Redwind Way
....3 B4
Lacy Close.........................3 A3
Lady Chapel Road 7 C5
Lady Downe Close 13 C2
Lady Margaret Court*,
    Lord Eldon Way 38 H3
Ladybellegate Street 16 F3
Ladysmith Road 6 E5
Ladywell Close 5 B4
Lake Side...........................36 F4
Lakers Road 17 D3
Lakeside Avenue 28 E4
Lakeside Drive...................28 E5
Lakeside Gardens 28 E4
Lamb Lane.........................34 F3
Lambourn Close 3 C6
Lambourne Avenue............39 D5
Lambsquay Road 19 D6/20 E5
Lampreys, The 6 H5
Lancaster Court..................27 B4
Lancaster Drive 27 B4
Lancaster Terrace 36 H4
Lancaster Way 37 D1
Langate*, Reservoir Road ...6 F6
Langdale Gardens 3 A4
Langetts Road....................19 D1
Langham House 38 G2
Langley Road 6 H6
Langton Close 7 C3
Lanham Gardens 10 H6
Lannett Road 6 E4/E5
Lansdown Road 2 F6
Lansdown Walk 23 B5
Lansdowne 34 E2
Lansdowne Cottages...........23 B5
Lansdowne Court 8 F5
Lantern Close 34 E3
Larches, The 7 C4
Larchwood Drive 12 E6
Lark Rise 17 C6
Larkfield Avenue 38 F2
Larkfield Park.....................38 E1
Larkham Close 12 H2
Larkham Place 12 H2
Larkhay Road 8 E2/E3
Larkhill Close 38 E2
Larksfield Road 31 D3
Larkspear Close 6 E6
Lassington Grove 9 A2
Lassington Lane 9 A2
Latimer Road 34 F2
Laura Close 2 H5
Laurel Farm Close 12 F1
Laurel Gate 13 D1
Laurel House*, Alexandra Road
....2 G6

Laureldene.........................20 E6
Laurels, The 6 F4
Lavender View....................13 D1
Lavington Drive 3 C5
Lawns, The (Glos.) 13 B2
Lawns, The*, Bristol Rd. 16 E6
Lawrence Way 16 F1
Lawrence Way North...........1 D5
Laxton Road 8 E5
Laymore Road....................33 D2
Laynes Road 8 E3/E4
Lea Crescent 3 A4
Leacey Court 4 E2
Leacey Mews.......................4 E2
Leaze Court 28 E4
Ledbury Road (Dymock) 39 C2
Ledbury Road (Newent).....36 F1
Ledbury Road (Staunton) ..40 E4
Ledbury Road Crescent......40 E4
Lensbrook 26 E6
Leominster Road 39 B1/C2
Leonard Road 6 F5
Lesanne Court 16 F4
Level, The 24 E4
Leven Close 3 B5
Lewis Avenue 2 F3
Lewis Glade 20 F1
Lewis Way 38 H3
Lewisham Road....................6 E6
Ley Court 7 D2
Lichfield Road 7 A3
Liddington Road 3 C6
Lights Place 23 A6
Lilac Way (Quedgeley) 10 G4
Lilac Way (Tuffley)..............11 C2
Lilliesfield Avenue 7 C3
Lime Court 3 D3
Lime Tree Court...................3 A6
Lime Way 27 C4
Limekiln Grove....................9 A1
Limes, The (Barnwood) 7 A2
Limes, The (Longford) 2 E4
Linden Close 38 G2
Linden Road 5 D4/D5
Linegar Wood Road............34 E6
Link Road...........................24 F3
Links, The 19 D2
Linnet Close 7 A6
Linsley Way 11 D4
Lion Close 10 H3
Listers Place 34 E3
Little Awefield 13 A1
Little Court 13 C3
Little Elmbridge 3 C5
Little Field 7 B4
Little Lancarridge 9 B2
Little Normans 3 A4
Little Walk 3 A4
Littledean Hill Road 34 G4
Littlefield 10 G3
Littleworth Court*, Brunswick Sq.
....16 F6
Livia Way 27 C4
Llandilo Street 16 H6
Llanthony Road.........5 C3/16 E4
Lloyd Baker Court 10 G6
Lobb Court 6 G2
Lobleys Drive 7 D6
Locks Row 20 F2
Lockvane Villas 24 G2
Lodge Gardens 21 C4
Lodge Walk 23 D4
Loiterpin 26 F1

London Road......................16 H2
Long Drive 18 F6
Long Field 9 B1
Longborough Drive 7 C6
Longbridge Cottages 39 C1
Longfield 10 G3
Longford Court 2 F2
Longford Lane 2 F3/G4
Longford Mews 2 F3
Longhope Close 7 C6
Longhope Road 39 A6
Longland Court 2 H4
Longland Gardens 2 H5
Longleat Avenue 11 C4
Longney Road 11 D2
Longsmith Street 16 F3
Longville Close 7 D6
Lonk, The 17 D3
Lonsdale Road 7 A1
Loop Road 38 F5
Lord Eldon Way..................38 H3
Lords Gate 19 D1
Lords Hill 19 D1
Lords Hill Close 19 D1
Loriners Close 10 H3
Lovage Close 3 D3
Lovett Close 40 F5
Lower Church Street 37 D3
Lower High Street*,
    Mornington Cres. 35 B5
Lower Lane 17 C5
Lower Meadow 10 H6
Lower Quay Street..............16 E2
Lower Rea..........................10 G2
Lower Ridge Walk 31 B2
Lower Road (Soudley).........35 B4
Lower Road (St. Brievals) ..21 B6
Lower Road (Yorkley).........24 G2
Lower Tuffley Lane 11 B1
Luke Lane 3 C3
Lych Gate Mews.........28 E3/F3
Lydfield Road 27 D3
Lydney Road 23 A6
Lyneham Drive 11 A5
Lyng Close 7 C3
Lynmouth Road 7 B2
Lynton Road 7 D4
Lynwood Road....................27 B3
Lypiatt Cottages 4 H6
Lysander Court 4 G4
Lysons Avenue 5 D4

M

Machen Road 18 F6
Madleaze Road 16 E6
Madocke Road 38 E4
Magdala Road 6 F2
Magdalen House 6 G1
Magnolia Close 38 G3
Magnolia Walk....................10 G3
Maidenhall 9 A1
Main Road (Huntley) 39 C5
Main Road (Mile End) 18 F5
Main Road (Pillowell)........24 F4
Mainard Square 3 A4
Maldon Gardens 6 F4
Malet Close 3 A4
Mallard Close 10 F4
Malmesbury Road 6 H4
Malvern Road (Glos.)...........2 F5
Malvern Road (Staunton) ..40 G4
Malvern Way 18 G2
Malverns, The 7 B5

Mandara Grove 13 B1
Mandeville Close 3 A4
Manley Gardens 3 A4
Mannings Road 31 D1
Manor Cottages (Glos.) 11 A6
Manor Cottages (Mitchdelean)
....40 F3
Manor Court (Glos.)............12 H1
Manor Court (Lydney) 27 D5
Manor Gardens (Glos.) 7 C3
Manor Gardens (Newnham)
....35 B6
Manor Park 3 C5
Manor Road.......................27 D5
Manor Way 37 D2
Manor, The 4 G5
Manse Road 31 D1
Mansell Close 5 C6
Mansfield Mews.................10 H6
Maple Avenue 38 G2
Maple Close 10 F5/G5
Maple Court 3 C5
Maple Drive 8 H4
Mapledean 34 E2
Maplefield 28 F1
Maples, The 7 C5
Marefield Close 7 C3
Marfells Way 30 H3
Margery Lane 19 B6/21 A2
Marian Court*, Priory Rd. ...5 D1
Marians Lane 17 C4
Marians Walk 17 C3
Marine Gardens 19 C1
Mariners Reach 38 H4
Marjoram Close 7 D6
Market Parade...................16 G3
Market Place 19 D1
Market Square...................36 G5
Market Street 34 F2
Marlborough Crescent.........6 G5
Marlborough Road 6 G4
Marleyfield Close 4 E2
Marleyfield Way 4 E2
Marram Close 7 D6
Marsh Hill..........................22 F1
Marsh Lane 22 F1
Marsh Road.......................38 G3
Marsh Way 22 E1
Marshalls Lane 34 F2
Marten Close 8 E6
Marten Road 38 F2
Martindale Road 4 F3
Martins, The 37 C4
Mary Grove 9 A1
Mary Rose Avenue 3 D2
Marylone 16 G3
Marys Lane 17 A6
Masefield Avenue 11 C1
Massey Parade*, Victory Road
....6 F4
Massey Road 6 G4
Mathern Road 38 F2/H1
Mathern Way......................6 G4
Matson Avenue 12 H3/13 A1
Matson Lane 12 H1/A2/13 A1
Matson Place 13 A1
Maverdine Court*, Clare Street
....16 E2
May Meadow Lane 40 F3
May Tree Square..................7 A4
Mayall Court 13 A2
Mayfair Close......................5 B3
Mayfield Drive 7 D3

Maypole·Green.....

Maypole Green 23 A5
Maypole Road 23 A5
Maze Walk.......................17 C3
Mead Lane 28 F1/G2
Mead Road 7 C5
Meadow Close 25 D3
Meadow Lane 37 D1
Meadow Road 34 G3
Meadow View 30 H3
Meadow Walk (Chepstow) .37 D1
Meadow Walk (Sling)........22 E1
Meadow Way 4 F3
Meadowbank 27 D5
Meadowcroft 7 C6
Meadowleaze 3 A6/B6
Meadowsweet Walk...........11 A4
Meads Close 17 C6
Meads Court 38 F2
Meadvale Close...................2 F3
Meend Gardens Terrace ...34 F4
Meend Lane 30 G2
Meendhurst Road 34 E3
Meerbrook Way 10 H6
Meerstone Way 13 B2
Melbourne Street East ..6 F4/G4
Melbourne Street West 6 F4
Melick Close 6 G6
Melody Way 3 B4
Melville Road 4 F4
Mendip Close 10 G5
Merchants Mead 10 F4
Merchants Road 16 E5
Mercia Road 16 F1
Mercian Way 38 E4
Mercury Way 7 D5
Meredith Cottages 6 H4
Merevale Road 2 H6
Merlin Drive 10 G3/H2
Merrin Street 40 F3
Merrin, The 40 F3
Merthyr Terrace 29 C6
Mertons, The 35 A6
Metz Way 6 F2/H3
Michaelmas Court 2 G6
Michaels Way 22 E1
Mickle Mead (Glos.) 7 C5
Mickle Mead (Highnam).......9 B1
Middle Court 36 G3
Middle Croft 7 B4
Middle Rea 10 H1
Middle Street 37 D2
Middle Way 38 G3
Middleton Lawn 3 C2
Midland Road 16 G6
Midsummer Walk.................5 C5
Mildenhall Way 11 B5
Mile End Road 18 E5
Miles Cottages 19 C6
Milestone Walk 22 E1
Milford Close 2 H4
Mill Court 36 G5
Mill End 40 F2
Mill Grove 10 F4
Mill House 31 C1
Mill Lane 37 D3
Mill Place 6 F4
Mill Row 29 B3
Mill Street 6 G2
Millbridge Road 8 E4
Millbrook Close 6 G2
Millbrook Green 28 F1
Millbrook Street 6 F3
Millend.............................26 G3

Millennium Cottages 40 F5
Miller Close 3 B4
Millers Close 31 B2
Millers Dyke 10 F4
Millers Way 34 E3
Millfields 8 E3
Millhill Lane 19 A4
Millin Avenue 11 D2
Millrough Cottages............27 B3
Millrough, The 27 B3
Milo Place 6 E5
Milton Avenue 5 C6/11 C1
Miners Walk 34 E3
Minerva Close 7 D5
Minerva Walk 27 B4
Minster Gardens 7 D5
Minstrel Way 3 D1
Mistletoe Mews*, Coriander Dr.
....3 D3
Moat House 12 H1
Moat Lane 40 F4
Moat, The 10 H4
Model Cottages 38 E5
Mogridge Close 8 E4
Monarch Close 13 C1
Monmouth Road 18 F3
Montfort Road 2 H4
Montgomery Close*, Folland Av.
....8 F5
Montpellier 16 F5/G5
Montpellier Close 23 C4
Montpellier Cottages 23 B4
Montpellier Mews*, Montpellier
....16 F5
Montpellier Road 23 B5/C4
Moor Street (Chepstow) 37 D2
Moor Street (Glos.) 6 F4
Moorend Cottages............13 D5
Moorhen Court 10 F4
Moorland Close 34 F2
Moorwood, The 29 D3
Mopla Cottages 37 B3
Mopla Road 37 B3
Morcroft Place 24 E4
Morelands Grove 6 E6
Moreton Street 6 F4
Morgans Lane 31 B3
Morgans Way 35 A1
Morgans Yard*, Alney Ter. ..1 C6
Mork Road 21 B4
Morley Avenue 4 E3
Morman Close 31 D1
Mornington Terrace 35 B5
Morpeth Street 6 F4
Morris Close 25 A2
Morse Fields 31 B1
Morse Lane 31 A1
Morse Road 31 A2/C3
Mortimer Road 2 H4
Morwent Close 7 C5
Moselle Drive 4 E3
Mostham Place 8 H5
Mottershead Drive 3 C2
Mount Close 31 D2
Mount Crete......................34 H3
Mount Pleasant (Chepstow)
....38 E2
Mount Pleasant (Glos.) 11 B4
Mount Pleasant (Lydney)...28 E5
Mount Pleasant (Parkend) ..24 F2
Mount Pleasant Close 28 E5
Mount Pleasant Cottages ..24 H2
Mount Pleasant Road 34 F4

Mount Street 16 F2
Mount Way....................37 C1/D1
Mountain View 30 G2
Mountjoys Lane 34 F2
Mountjoys Lane End 34 F2
Mounton Close 38 E1
Mounton Drive 38 E1
Mounton Road 38 E1
Mousell Lane 34 F3
Mousell Villas 34 F4
Mowberry Close 3 A4
Moyle Old School Lane 37 A4
Mulberry Close 10 G5
Munsley Grove 13 A2
Mushet Place 19 C2
Mushet Walk 19 D1
Mutlers Row 32 G2
Mutsilver Mews 3 C4
Myers Road 6 G2
Myrtle Close 6 G6
Myrtle Place 37 D3
Myrtle Villas 29 C6
Myrtles, The 37 C4
Mythe Terrace 35 A5

N

Naas Court........................28 F6
Naas Lane (Glos.).....10 H6/11 A6
Naas Lane (Lydney) 27 D4/28 E6
Nags Head Cottages.........19 B3
Nailsmiths Court 34 H3
Nanfan & Dobyn Place 36 F4
Napier Street 6 F2
Nash Way 19 D2
Nature Close 8 H6
Naunton Road 7 A4
Needham Avenue 11 B6
Nelson Street (Chepstow) ..37 D2
Nelson Street (Glos.) 6 F5
Nene Close 10 G3
Neptune Close 7 D5
Nero Close 27 C5
Netheridge Close 11 A1
Nettleton Road 16 H4
New Inn Lane 16 G3
New Mills 27 B3
New Road (Aylburton)
....................................24 E4/27 A2
New Road (Blakeney) 25 D2
New Road (Bream) 22 H5
New Road (Cinderford) 34 H3
New Road (Coalway)..........20 F2
New Road (Lydbrook) 29 C6
New Road (Mitcheldean) 40 F3
New Road (Parkend) 24 E1/E2
New Road (Whitecroft) 24 G3
New Street (Glos.) 16 F6
New Street (Mitcheldean) ..40 F3
Newark House*, Hempsted Lane
....5 B5
Newark Road 5 C5
Newent Lane 39 B4
Newerne Street 27 D3
Newland Street (Coleford) .19 C2
Newland Street (Glos.) 6 F1
Newlands Court.................36 G5
Newnham Road 34 H4
Newport Road 38 E1/F1
Newsham House*, Stroud Road
....16 F6
Newstead Road 7 C3
Newton Avenue 7 A4
Newton Close 39 C5

Newton House*, London Road
....16 H2
Newtown Road 31 D5
Nexus Court 14 H1
Nickleby Bungalows............6 F6
Nicolson Close 3 C2
Nightingale Croft 3 B3
Nightingale House 13 B1
Nine Elms Road 3 C5
Nine Wells Close 17 D3
Nine Wells Road 17 D3
Noake Road 8 E3
Nodens Way 27 C5
Norbury Avenue 6 H6/12 H1
Norfolk Mews*, Norfolk St...16 F4
Norfolk Street 16 F4
Norman Ball Way 6 H2
Norman Way 30 G1
Normandy Way 37 C1
Normansland Road 39 B3
Norse Way 38 E5
North Avenue 31 D1
North Point.......................16 E4
North Road (Broadwell) 18 F5
North Road (Glos.)..............2 F6
North Road (Huntley) 39 C5
North Upton Lane 7 C4
North Villas 16 F5
Northbrook Road 7 A2
Northern Way 40 G2
Northfield Road 6 F6
Northfield Square 6 F6
Northgate Street 16 G3
Northwood Close 34 F2
Notgrove Close 11 C3
Notley Place 8 E4
Nourse Place 40 F3
Nourse Place*, New Rd. 40 F3
Nut Croft 6 H4
Nuthill 13 D3/14 F3
Nutley Avenue 11 C3
Nutmeg Close 13 B1
Nympsfield Road 11 C2

O

Oak Close 38 G2
Oak Cottages 8 H4
Oak Dean..........................24 F4
Oak Drive 8 H5
Oak Field, The 34 G3
Oak House 8 H5
Oak Lane 24 F3
Oak Meadow 27 A4
Oak Terrace.......................35 B5
Oak Tree Close 10 G5
Oak Villas (Glos.) 4 G4
Oak Villas (Lydbrook) 29 C6
Oak Villas (Yorkley) 25 A2
Oak Way (Huntley) 39 B4
Oak Way (Littledean)........34 H3
Oakbank 12 E1
Oakcroft Close 13 B3
Oakdean 34 E2
Oakfield Avenue 37 D1
Oakfield Gardens 23 D1
Oakfields 19 C1
Oakhill Road 40 F2
Oakhurst Close 3 D4
Oakland Road 31 D3
Oaklands Park 23 D4
Oaklands Walk 22 E1
Oaklea Road 25 A2
Oakleaze 3 B6

Oakley Way 23 A6
Oakridge..........................9 B1/B2
Oakridge Close 13 C1
Oaks, The 7 C4/C5
Oaktree Cottages..............30 F4
Oaktree Gardens 13 A2
Oakwood Close (Bream) ...23 A4
Oakwood Close (Cinderford)
..................................34 F2
Oakwood Drive 7 D5
Oakwood Road (Bream) ...23 A4
Oakwood Road (Sling) 20 E6
Oatfield 10 G3
Octagon, The 38 G3
Octavia Place 27 C4
Offas Close 38 E4
Office Road 34 E4
Ogbourne Close 3 D2
Old Bear Buildings, The*,
Severn Street 35 B6
Old Bulwark Road 38 E2
Old Cheltenham Road..........3 A5
Old Court.........................36 G5
Old Dam Road...................25 A6
Old Dean Road 40 F1
Old Elmore Lane 10 H3
Old Furnace Close...........28 E2
Old George Cottages*,
Stars Pitch 40 F2
Old Hill............................37 C3
Old Maids Walk 36 F4
Old Oak Close 38 G3
Old Painswick Close 6 H5
Old Painswick Road 6 H5
Old Road (Coalway) 20 F1/F2
Old Road (Maisemore) 1 A2
Old Row 6 F3
Old Row Court*, Old Row ...6 F3
Old Station Road 36 F4
Old Station Way 19 D1
Old Town Mews 28 E2
Old Tram Road 16 F4
Old Tree Heart, The 31 D1
Old Vicarage Court 19 D1
Old Yorkley Cottages 24 G3
Oldbury Gardens 4 H5
Oldbury Orchard 4 H5
Oldcroft 25 A3
Oldcroft Road 25 A3
Oliver Close 11 D3
Olympus Park 11 A3
Onslow Road.....................36 G5
Orangery, The 7 C4
Orchard Avenue 38 G2
Orchard Close (Coleford) ...19 B6
Orchard Close (Hardwicke) 10 F6
Orchard Close (Longford) 2 E4
Orchard Close (Mitcheldean)
..................................40 F2
Orchard Close (Woodcroft) 37 A4
Orchard Cottages 29 A3
Orchard Drive 4 H5
Orchard Farm Close 38 E5
Orchard Gardens 37 C3
Orchard Gate 26 F3
Orchard Mobile Home Park..2 H1
Orchard Park 8 E5
Orchard Rise 35 A6
Orchard Road (Coleford) ...17 D6
Orchard Road (Glos.) 3 C5
Orchard Road (Lydbrook) ..29 C4
Orchard Road (Lydney) 28 E4
Orchard Road (Newent)....36 F1

Orchard Way (Berry Hill) 17 D3
Orchard Way (Glos.) 4 F2
Orchard Way (Huntley) 39 D4
Orchard Way (Maisemore) ...1 A2
Orchards, The (Glos.) 8 E5
Orchards, The (Lydney) 27 D3
Organs Alley*, Russell St...16 G3
Oriole Way..........................7 A5
Ormerod Road..................38 E4
Osborne Avenue 11 C4
Osier Close 12 G1
Osprey Close 7 B6
Osric Road..........................6 F5
Otter Road..........................7 D6
Otterburn House 11 C1
Oval, The 5 D5/D6
Over Causeway 1 B6
Overbrook Close 7 A2
Overbrook Road 10 G5
Overbury Road 6 G3
Owen Gardens 17 C6
Owl Close 7 B6
Owls Eye Close 18 F5
Oxebode, The 16 G3
Oxford Road 16 H2
Oxford Street (Chepstow) ..37 D2
Oxford Street (Glos.) 16 H2
Oxford Street (Lydney) 28 E3
Oxford Terrace 16 H3
Oxmoor 13 B1/B2
Oxstalls Drive 2 G4
Oxstalls Lane 2 H5
Oxstalls Way 2 H5

P

Packers Road 34 F3
Paddock Gardens 3 B4
Paddock, The (Chepstow) ..38 F1
Paddock, The (Highnam)......9 A2
Paddocks, The (Coleford) ..18 E6
Painswick Road (Brockworth)
.............................14 G6/H4
Painswick Road (Glos.) ..6 G4/H5
Painswick Road (Matson) ..13 A1
Palmer Avenue 7 D6
Parade, The (Brockworth) ...8 H6
Parade, The (Glos.) 3 C5
Parawell Lane 22 G6
Park Avenue 3 A4
Park Brake 9 B2
Park Close 21 C5
Park Court 27 D3
Park Drive 10 H4
Park End Road 16 G6
Park Farm Cottages 30 G1
Park Grove 23 D4
Park Hill 23 D4
Park Lane 21 D6
Park Road (Berry Hill) 17 C3
Park Road (Coleford) 17 D6
Park Road (Glos.) 16 G4
Park Street 16 G2
Park View (Chepstow) 37 C1
Park View (Ruardean) 30 H1
Park View (Sedbury) 37 D5
Parkend Cottages 15 A5
Parkend Road (Bream)
...........................23 B1/B2/B3
Parkend Road (Coalway) ...20 F2
Parkend Road (Yorkley) 24 G1
Parkend Walk (Coalway)
..........................20 F2/F3
Parkend Walk (Coleford) 19 D4

Parkend Walk (Sling)..........22 E1
Parklands (Churchdown)......3 D3
Parklands (Glos.) 10 G4
Parks Road 40 G3
Parkside 19 D1
Parkside Close 3 D3
Parkside Drive 3 D3
Parkwood Crescent.....7 D5/8 E5
Parliament Street 16 F4
Parr Close 3 D2
Parragate 34 E2
Parragate Road 34 E2
Parry Road 6 F5
Parton Drive 4 G4
Parton Mews 4 F3
Parton Road 4 E2/G4
Partridge Close 5 C6
Pastors Hill 23 B5
Patches, The 30 H3
Patseamur Mews...............3 C4
Paul Street 6 F4
Pauls Walk 39 C4
Paygrove Lane 3 B5
Paynes Pitch 4 H6
Peacock Close (Glos.).......7 C6
Peacock Close (Newent) ...36 F5
Peacock Gardens 36 F5
Peacock Lane 34 E6
Pear Tree Close 10 G6
Pearce Way 11 B1
Peart Close 6 G2
Pearwood Way 11 C3
Pegasus Court 7 C2
Pegasus Gardens 10 H3
Peggotty Bungalows 7 A4
Pelham Crescent................4 E3
Pembroke Road 38 G2
Pembroke Street (Cinderford)
..................................34 F3
Pembroke Street (Glos.) ..16 H5
Pembury Road..................12 E1
Penby Lawn......................35 A6
Penda Place 38 E4
Pendock Close 10 G4
Penhill House*, Penhill Road
..................................12 H1
Penhill Road 12 H1
Penmoel Cottages 37 A3
Penmoel Lane 37 A4
Penmoyle Gardens 37 A4
Pennine Close 10 G5
Penny Close 3 B5
Pennywell Lane 34 H4
Penrose Road 3 B3
Penterry Park 37 D1
Perch Close 18 G5
Perch Drive 18 G5
Percy Street 6 F4
Peregrine Close 10 H2
Perry Close 36 G5
Perry Orchard 13 C3
Perrygrove Road 20 E4
Perrygrove Road.....19 D3/20 E4
Perrys Court Lane 30 F1
Persch Way 1 A2
Persh Farm Cottages 1 A3
Persh Lane 1 A2
Peters Field 9 B1
Petty Marsh 21 C6
Pettycroft 30 G2
Petworth Close 11 C5
Peveril House 11 C1
Philip Street 16 E6

Philips Close 25 B4
Phoenix Court 19 C1
Phoenix Drive 38 H3
Picklenash Court 36 E4
Pickwick Close....................3 B6
Picton House 16 H2
Piece, The 4 G5
Piercefield Avenue 37 C1
Pike Road 17 D6
Pilgrim Close 7 C5
Pillowell Drive 6 G1
Pillowell Road 24 E4
Pillows Green Road...........40 H4
Pincoate...........................9 B1
Pine Crest Way 23 A5
Pine Tree Drive 7 C3
Pine Tree Way..................25 D3
Pine Way 6 H5
Pineholt Gate 8 F5
Pinemount Road 8 E4
Pinery Road........................7 C4
Pinewood Close 34 G2
Pinewood Road 10 G5
Pingry Lane 19 B5
Pinlocks 13 C2
Pintail Close 10 F4
Pipers Grove 9 A1
Pippin Close (Glos.)............8 E5
Pippin Close (Newent) 36 G5
Pirton Court 4 F4
Pirton Crescent 4 F4
Pirton Lane 4 E3
Pirton Meadow 4 F4
Pitch View*, Kingsholm Road
..................................16 G1
Pitt Mill Gardens 8 E3
Pitt Street 16 F2
Place de Cormeilles 37 D2
Plantation, The (Glos.).........7 B5
Plantation, The (Hardwicke)
..................................10 F6
Platts Row*, High Street 40 F2
Pleasant Stile 34 H4
Plock Court 2 F4
Ploughmans Way 15 C1
Pludds Court Road 30 E4
Plumtree Close 13 C1
Pochard Close 10 F4
Podsmead Court 11 D1
Podsmead Place 5 D6
Podsmead Road 5 D6/11 C1
Pollards Lane....................26 E4
Pool Meadow Caravan Park 1 C6
Poole Ground 9 B1
Poolway Court 19 D1
Poolway Place 19 D1
Poolway Rise 17 D6
Poolway Road 18 E6
Popes Meade 9 B2
Poplar Close 11 D1
Poplar Way 10 G6
Poplars, The (Lydbrook) ...29 C5
Poplars, The (Tutshill) 37 C2
Poppy Field 9 B1
Porchester Road 7 D4
Portwall Road 38 E2
Portway 13 D4/14 F6
Post Offices Cottages 29 A3
Posy Lane 2 G6
Potters Croft 38 H5
Pound Close 14 H1
Pound Farm Courtyard 8 H6
Pound Lane 15 A2

Prescott Avenue 12 H1
Preston Close 38 H3
Price Street 16 E6
Prices Ground 7 B5
Priday Mills*, Commercial Road
....16 E3
Primrose Close 12 G1
Primrose Drive...................20 E4
Primrose Hill Road 27 C3
Primrose Way 27 B3
Prince Albert Court 8 G5
Prince Crescent.................40 F5
Prince Street 16 H4
Princes Mews 3 D2
Princess Royal Road 23 B4
Prinknash 13 A1
Prinknash Close 13 A1
Prinknash Road 13 A1
Priory Close........................37 C1
Priory Court 4 H4
Priory Place 16 F4
Priory Road 16 E2/F2
Priory, The.........................37 D3
Proberts Barn Lane 29 A4
Prospect Close 19 D1
Prospect Cottages (Blakeney)
....26 F2
Prospect Cottages (Tutshill)
....37 B3
Prospect Cottages (Woodcroft)
....37 A4
Prospect Road...................34 F3
Prospect Terrace..................5 A5
Prosper Lane 20 F2
Prosper Villas 20 G2
Pullman Court*, Gt. Western Rd.
....16 H2
Purcell Road 4 E1
Purples, The 20 G1
Purslane 12 H1
Purton Place 28 E5
Puslane Close 12 H1
Putts Alley 36 F5
Puzzle Close 23 A5
Pyart Court 19 D1
Pylers Way 28 E4
Pystol Lane 21 C4

Q

Quabbs Cottages 31 D2
Quabbs Lane 31 C2
Quail Close 7 C4
Quantock Road 10 G5
Quay Street 16 E2
Quay, The 16 E3
Quedgeley Court Park........11 A2
Quedgeley District Centre ..11 A4
Quedgeley Park*, Greenhill Drive
....11 E2
Queen Street......................27 C4
Queens Acre 35 A6
Queens Close 8 E2
Queens Road 38 F2
Queens Walk*, Eastgate Precinct
....16 G3
Queensway 20 F1
Quenneys Close 13 A2
Quinton Close 4 F3

R

Raglan Gardens 27 D3
Raglan Street.......................6 F2
Raglan Way........................38 G3

Raikes Road 5 D5
Railway Cottages 23 D1
Railway Drive 19 D1
Railway Road 34 E6
Railway Terrace 28 G3
Raleigh Close 3 D1
Ram Row 30 G3
Ramsdale Road..................11 B2
Rance Pitch 13 C3
Randwick Road 11 D3
Range, The 9 B1
Ranmoor 13 B2
Ravis Close 6 H5
Rea Lane 5 A6
Rea, The 10 H1
Rectory Close 13 C3
Rectory Lane 5 A5
Rectory Road.....................13 A1
Red Admiral Drive 13 C1
Red Lion Court 6 G3
Red Well Road 12 H3
Redding Close....................10 G4
Reddings Lane 34 G3
Reddings, The (Chepstow) 38 G3
Reddings, The (Lydbrook)..29 D4
Redland Close 2 H5
Redlands Acre*,
    Tewkesbury Road 2 F4
Redlands Court*,
    Tewkesbury Road 2 F4
Redmarley Road 36 F3
Redpoll Way 7 A5
Redstart Way.......................7 A5
Redwind Way 3 B4
Redwood Close (Chepstow)
....38 G2
Redwood Close (Glos.) 5 D6
Redwood House*,
    Gt. Western Road 16 H3
Reevers Road 36 G5
Regent Street (Glos.) 16 G6
Regent Street (Lydney) 27 D3
Regent Way.......................37 D2
Regents Court 27 D4
Regents Walk*, Newerne Street
....27 D3
Remus Close 7 D5
Rendcomb Close................13 C1
Reservoir Road 6 F6/12 E1
Restway Wall......................37 D2
Retreat, The*, Bristol Rd....16 E6
Ribston Mews 6 E6
Richmond Avenue 7 A5
Richmond Gardens 3 A4
Richmonds, The 13 A1
Ridge Place........................30 G5
Ridgemount Close...............8 H5
Ridgemount Court 8 E1
Ridgeway 25 A2
Ridings, The 1 A2
Ridler Road 28 E5
Riflemans Way 37 D2
Rissington Road 12 E3
River View 37 D2
Rivermead Close 2 E4/E5
Riverside Mill......................37 C3
Riversley Road 6 H1
Robert Raikes Avenue 11 D3
Roberts Road 3 C2
Robin Hood Junction 17 A5
Robinhood Street................16 E6
Robins End 3 B2
Robins Wood Hill.................6 G6

Robinson Close 36 F4
Robinson Lane 29 C6
Robinson Road 5 D4/6 E4
Robinswood Gardens 12 G1
Robinswood House*,
    Gt. Western Road 16 H3
Robinswood Place*, Matson Av.
....13 A1
Rock Cottages 21 B6
Rock Lane 19 C2
Rock Villa Lane 37 C3
Rock Villas 31 C1
Rockleigh Close..................12 E2
Rocks Road 29 B3/C3
Rocks, The 19 D6
Rockwood Cottages 38 E3
Rockwood Road 38 E2
Rodley Road 27 D4
Rodley Square....................27 D5
Rodney Close 2 H5
Roebuck Meadows 30 H3
Roman Quay House*, Quay St.
....16 E2
Roman Road 7 C5
Roman Way (Cinderford) ..34 H3
Roman Way (Coleford) 19 D2
Roman Way (Glos.)..............8 H5
Romney Close 6 E6
Rookery Lane 19 A6/21 A1
Rookery Road 3 A3
Rose Cottages (Glos.)..........6 G2
Rose Cottages (Lydbrook)..29 B3
Rose Cottages (Milkwall) 20 F3
Rose Cottages (St. Briavels)
....21 D5
Rose Cottages (Viney Hill) 25 C3
Rosebank*, Stroud Road....16 F6
Rosebery Avenue 6 E6
Rosedale Close 10 F5
Rosemary Close 13 A1
Rosewood 34 E2
Ross Road (Coleford) 17 C2
Ross Road (Huntley) 39 A4
Ross Road (Mitcheldean) ..40 F1
Ross Road (Newent) 36 E4
Ross Willis Court................36 G5
Rougemont Grove 38 H3
Rowan Close 38 G2
Rowan Drive 38 G2
Rowan Gardens 8 H4
Rowandean 34 E2
Royal Lane...........................6 F1
Royal Oak Road (Glos.) 16 E2
Royal Oak Road (The Pludds)
....30 F4
Ruardean Road...................30 G3
Rudge, The (Maisemore)......1 B1
Rudge, The (Yorkley) 24 G3
Rudhall Court......................16 E2
Ruffet Close (Coleford) 19 D3
Ruffets Close (Chepstow) .37 D1
Ruffitt, The..........................34 H2
Rumsey Close 13 C1
Rushes, The 11 A3
Rushyleaze 28 E4
Ruspidge Close 7 C6
Ruspidge Road 35 A2
Russell Street 16 G3
Russet Close 11 B2
Russett Way 36 G5
Rustic Close 7 A6
Rydal Road 2 H5
Ryder Row 3 C3

Rye Cottages 37 A5
Ryecroft Street 16 H5
Ryelands 11 C2
Ryelands Road 23 B5
Ryton Road 39 D2

S

Sabrina Way 27 C4
Saddlers Road 10 H3
Saffron Close 6 G6
Sage Close 3 D3
Saintbridge Close 6 H6
Saintbridge House*,
    Painswick Road 6 H5
Saintbridge Place 6 H6
Salisbury Road 6 G4
Salvia Close 3 D3
San Remo 6 E5
Sandalwood Drive 5 B4
Sandfield Court 4 G4
Sandfield Road 4 H5
Sandford Way 11 B3
Sandhurst Lane.............1 D2/2 E4
Sandhurst Road...................2 E5
Sandpiper Close 10 F4
Sandringham Avenue 11 C4
Sandstar Close 3 B4
Sandy Lane 21 B6
Sandycroft Road 4 E2
Sandyleaze 3 A6/B6
Sapperton Road...................1 B6
Sapphire Close 11 B3
Sarnedy Road 19 D1
Saturn Close 7 D5
Saunders Green 23 C4
Savernake Road 6 G4
Saw Mills End 7 B2
Saxon Close 3 A4
Saxon Place 38 E4
Sayers Crescent 8 H6
Saylittle Mews 3 C4
Scarr, The 36 F1
Scholars Walk 10 H4
School Close 20 F1
School Cottages 19 C6
School Crescent (Lydbrook)
....29 C4
School Crescent (Lydney) ..27 B4
School Crescent (Staunton)
....40 G5
School Hill 37 D2
School Lane (Hardwicke)
.................................10 F5/G5
School Lane (Ruardean) 30 F2
School Mews 12 H1
School Road (Joy's Green)
....29 C3/C4
School Road (Pillowell) 24 E4
School Road (Ruardean) ..30 G1
School Road (Up. Lydbrook)
....29 C5
Scott Avenue 11 C1
Scott House*, Southgate Street
....16 E3
Scowles Road 17 A6/19 A1
Seabroke Road (Glos.) 2 F6
Seabrook Road (Brockworth)
....8 H6
Sebert Street 2 F6
Secunda Way 5 B5
Sedbury Lane (Sedbury)
.................................37 C5/D5
Sedbury Lane (Tutshill) 37 C3

Sedgeley Close 11 C3
Sellars Road 10 F6
Selwyn Road 6 F6
Serlo Road 16 G1
Seven Acres 7 B4
Seven Stars Road 34 E1
Seventh Avenue 11 D3
Severn Avenue 37 C4
Severn Bridge Park Homes
....38 G5
Severn Bridge, The 38 H3
Severn Close 1 B2
Severn Crescent 38 E2
Severn Lodge*, Matson Lane
....13 A1
Severn Oaks 10 H6
Severn Road (Glos.) 16 E4
Severn Road (Lydney).......28 E4
Severn Street....................35 B6
Severn Terrace 35 B6
Severn View (Chepstow)...37 D1
Severn View (Cinderford) .34 G2
Severn View Road 25 A2
Severnbank Avenue 27 D5
Severnvale Drive...............10 G5
Seymour Close 17 C3
Seymour Road 5 D5
Shackleton Close................4 F4
Shakespeare Avenue ..11 C1/C2
Shamrock Close 3 D3
Sharps Way*, Summer Ho. Lane
....38 G3
Shearwater Grove 3 B3
Sheens Meadow 35 A5
Sheevaun Close 3 B4
Shelduck Road 10 E4
Shelley Avenue 11 C1
Shepherd Road 11 B2
Shepherds Way (Glos.).......3 D2
Sheppard Way (Newent)...36 H5
Sherborne House 16 H2
Sherborne Street 16 H2
Shergar Close 13 B1
Sherwood Green 2 F3
Shophouse Road...............21 D2
Sidney Street 6 G2
Silcock Close 3 D2
Silleys Close 37 B3
Silver Birch Close 10 G4
Silver Close 11 C2
Silver Street (Cinderford) ..34 H4
Silver Street (Mitcheldean) 40 F3
Silverdale Parade 7 D3
Simmonds Road 7 D5
Simon Road.........................3 A4
Sims Lane 10 H1/H2
Sinope Street 6 F2
Sisson End 7 B1
Sisson Road 7 A1
Sivell Close 2 G3
Six Acres 13 D2
Skinner Street 16 G2
Skylark Way 6 H6
Slade Road 24 H2
Slaney Street 6 F4
Slimbridge Road 11 D2
Smiths Hill 20 G5
Smithville Close................21 D4
Smithville Place 21 D4
Smithy, The 26 G2
Smithyman Court 35 B5
Snead Park 7 D6

Sneedhams Green 12 H4
Sneedhams Road 12 H3
Snowdon Gardens 4 E2
Snowdrop Close 7 C6
Snowshill Close...................7 C4
Soldiers Walk 4 F6
Somerset Cottages 37 C3
Somerset Place 16 F5
Somerset Road 34 E3
Somerset Way...................38 H3
Soren Larsen Way..............5 B5
Sorrel Close 12 G1
South Close.........................2 H5
South Point 16 E4
South Road (Coalway).......20 F1
South Road (Coleford) 17 C6
South Road (Lydney) 27 C3
South View 37 C4
South Walk 40 G2
Southbrook Road.................7 A2
Southend Lane 36 F6
Southern Avenue..............12 E1
Southfield Road (Coleford) 17 D6
Southfield Road (Glos.).....12 E1
Southgate Street...........16 F4/F5
Southwood Close..............34 F2
Sovereign Chase...............40 G5
Sovereign Court 6 F1
Spa Mews 16 F5
Spa Road 16 F5
Spa Villas 16 G5
Sparrowhill........................17 C6
Spartan Close 7 C5
Speculation Road 31 D6
Speech House Road
...............................18 F6/33 A6
Speedwell 18 F5
Speedwell Close 7 C6
Spencer Close 7 D4
Spey Close 10 H3
Spinnaker Road..................5 B3
Spinney Road 7 C4
Spire Way 7 B3
Spoonbill Close 10 F4
Spout Lane (Plump Hill) ...32 H4
Spout Lane (Rua. Hill) 31 A2
Spread Eagle Court...........16 G3
Spread Eagle Road...........16 G3
Spring Lane Cottages 9 A3
Spring Meadow Road........27 C3
Spring Place 30 F2
Springdale Close 10 F5
Springfield.........................10 G6
Springfield Close 19 D1
Springfield Drive...............34 E1
Springfield Road 27 C3
Springs, The 27 D3
Springwell Gardens 4 F2
Spruce Road 18 F5
Square, The (Huntley).......39 C5
Square, The (Ruardean) ...30 F1
Square, The (St. Briavels) ..21 C4
Squires Road 29 B5
Squirrel Close 10 G6
St. Albans Road 5 C6
St. Aldate Street 16 G3
St. Aldwyn Road 6 F5
St. Andrews Avenue 38 E2
St. Ann Street 37 C3
St. Ann Way......................16 E5
St. Annals Road 34 F3
St. Annes Close..................8 H5
St. Annes Way...................21 C4

St. Anns Cross...................23 A5
St. Barnabas Close 12 E1
St. Bartholomews (Newent)
....36 G5
St. Bartholomews*, Belgrave Rd.
....16 G5
St. Bruels Close.................21 C4
St. Catherine Court*,
   Wheatstone Road 6 E4
St. Catherine Street...........16 G1
St. Davids Close (Chepstow)
....38 E2
St. Davids Close (Glos.) 11 C2
St. Ewens Road 38 F2
St. Francis Way 3 B3
St. George Road (Chepstow)
....38 E2
St. Georges Close 11 C2
St. Georges Road (Brockworth)
....8 H6
St. Georges Way 38 H5
St. Giles Court 1 A2
St. James 10 H4
St. James Close 10 H4
St. James Mews*, Upton Street
....6 G3
St. James Park 20 E5
St. James Square 22 H6
St. James Street 6 F3
St. Johns Avenue 4 E3
St. Johns Court*, St. Johns St.
....19 D1
St. Johns Gardens.............37 C1
St. Johns Lane 16 G3
St. Johns Road 30 G1
St. Johns Square 34 E5
St. Johns Street 19 D1
St. Josephs Travellers Park
....15 A5
St. Kilda Parade 16 H4
St. Kingsmark Avenue.......37 C1
St. Lawrence Lane.............38 E1
St. Lawrence Parc.............37 D1
St. Lawrence Road (Chepstow)
....37 C1/E1
St. Lawrence Road (Glos.) ..7 B4
St. Leonards Close 13 C3
St. Leonards Court 13 C3
St. Lucys Court 16 G2
St. Luke Street..................16 E5
St. Margarets Road (Glos.) ..7 D3
St. Margarets Road (Ruardean)
....30 G1
St. Margarets*, London Road
....16 H2
St. Mark Street 16 G1
St. Marks Court 16 H1
St. Marks*, Sherborne St. ..16 H2
St. Mary Street (Chepstow)37 D2
St. Marys Close (Dymock) ..39 B2
St. Marys Close (Glos.) 16 F2
St. Marys Square (Glos.) ...16 F2
St. Marys Square (Lydney) 27 D5
St. Marys Street (Glos.) 16 F2
St. Maur Gardens 37 C1
St. Michaels Buildings*,
   Eastgate Street 16 G3
St. Michaels Close 40 F2
St. Michaels Court*,
   St. Michaels Square....16 G4
St. Michaels Square 16 G4
St. Nicholas Court (Hardwicke)
....10 G6

St. Nicholas Court*,
   Archdeacon Street 16 F2
St. Nicholas Square*,
   Westgate Street 16 E2
St. Oswalds Road 16 E2
St. Patricks Court 8 H6
St. Pauls Court 16 G6
St. Pauls Road 16 F6
St. Peters Close................35 B6
St. Peters Road 13 A2
St. Philips Close 8 E2
St. Philips Court 16 F6
St. Stephens Court 5 D4
St. Swithins Road (Oldcroft)
....25 B4
St. Swithins Road (Glos.) ...5 A5
St. Tecla Road 38 F2
St. Tewdric Road 38 F2
St. Vincent Way 4 E1
St. Whites Court 34 E5
St. Whites Road................34 E5
St. Whites Terrace 34 E5
Stafford Close 18 F6
Stable Mews 19 D1
Stag Hill 24 G2
Staites Orchard 13 C2
Stampers Row 24 E2
Stamps Meadow 2 F4
Stanbridge Way 11 A5
Stanbury Mews 8 F5
Stanford Road 27 D3
Stank Lane 15 A1
Stanleigh Terrace 1 A2
Stanley Cottages 6 F3
Stanley Flats 31 C2
Stanley Road 6 E5
Stanley Terrace 6 E4
Stanley Walk 13 D4
Stanley, The 13 D3
Stanmoor 13 B2
Stansby Crescent 4 E3
Stansted House*, Priory Road
....16 D2
Stanway Road 7 A4
Stars Pitch 40 F2
Station Approach...............16 H3
Station Close.......................4 H4
Station Road (Chepstow) ..37 D2
Station Road (Churchdown)
....4 G3/G5
Station Road (Coleford).....20 E4
Station Road (Glos.) ...16 G3/H3
Station Road (Lydney) 28 F3
Station Road (Newnham) ..35 A5
Station Street....................34 E2
Station Terrace (Cinderford)
....34 E2
Station Terrace (Dymock) ..39 B2
Station Villas 26 F3
Staunton Close 13 C1
Staunton Road...17 A4/A5/19 C1
Steam Mills Road 31 D5/34 E1
Steel Avenue 27 D4
Steep Street......................38 E2
Steeple Close 7 B3
Steeple View 28 E3
Stenders Court*, Stenders Road
....40 F2
Stenders Road 40 F3
Stenders, The 40 E3
Stepbridge Road 20 E3
Stephens Place 18 F6
Stevans Close 2 G4

Stewarts Mill Lane 13 C1
Sticky Lane 15 C1
Stirling Way 11 B3
Stirrup Close 5 B5
Stockdale Close.................10 F5
Stocken Close 8 F5
Stockley Way 13 B6
Stockwell Green 34 E4/F4
Stone Close (Bream) 23 A5
Stone Close (Glos.) 7 C4
Stone Close (Mile End) 18 F5
Stone Road, The 40 F5
Stonebrack Piece 7 B5
Stonechat Avenue 7 A6
Stonehenge Road 6 H4
Stoney Bridge 7 C5
Stoney Field.......................9 B1
Stoulgrove Lane 37 A4
Stow Close...........................6 F6
Stowe Lane 21 A3
Stowell Mews.......................7 B4
Stowfield Cottages...........29 A2
Stowfield Road 29 A2/A3
Straight Lane...................40 G4
Strand, The*, London Road
....16 H2
Stratford Close 11 C1
Strathmore Estate 20 E6
Stratton Corner*, Stratton Road
....6 F3
Stratton Road.......................6 F3
Strawberry Field 17 C3
Strawberry Hill..................36 G1
Stray Court 13 C2
Streamside 11 A3
Striguil Road 38 G2
Strongbow Road 38 F2
Stroud Road (Glos.)..........16 F6
Stroud Road (Tuffley) 12 E4
Stuart Avenue 37 C1
Stump Lane 8 F3
Sudbrook Way.....................6 H6
Sudgrove Park 7 C6
Sudmeadow Road 5 B2
Suffolk House*, Eastgate Street
....16 G4
Sulgrave Close 11 C4
Summer Court....................26 G3
Summer House Lane 38 H3
Summer Meadow*, Norbury Av.
....12 H1
Summerland Drive 4 G4
Summerleaze 28 E4
Summerleaze Road...........28 E4
Sun Green Close 23 A4
Sun Green Road 23 A4
Sun Lane 18 F6
Sun Rise Road 23 A4
Sun Tump 23 A5
Sunderland Court 4 G4
Sunny Bank (Coleford) 17 C6
Sunnybank (High Nash) ...19 D2
Sunnybank Road...............17 C6
Sunnycroft Mews.................6 E6
Sunnyfield Road 10 F5
Sunnyhill Road*,
   Forest View Park 34 E4
Sunnymead Close.............31 D1
Sunnyside 23 A4
Sunnyside Cottages (Lydbrook)
....29 D6
Sunnyside Cottages (Woodcroft)
....37 A4

Sunnyside Cottages*,
   Sweetbriar Street 2 F6
Sunnyside Cottages*, Guinea St.
....16 H1
Sunset Place 39 C5
Sunview Cottages 29 B4
Sussex Gardens 8 F4
Sutton Road (Cinderford) ..34 H5
Sutton Road (Soudley) 35 B3
Swallow Crescent...........3 B2/B3
Swan Court 16 E2
Swan Lane 26 G2
Swan Road (Glos.) 16 H1
Swan Road (Lydney)........27 D3
Sweetbriar Street 16 G1
Swift Road 7 B6
Swinley Cottages...................1 A2
Swish Lane 31 B1
Swordfish Close 4 G4
Sybil Road 6 F5
Sycamore Avenue 38 G2
Sycamore Close 5 D6
Sycamore Road.................31 D3
Sydenham Terrace 6 E4
Sylvan Close 19 D2

T

Tainmor Close 3 C4
Talbot Mews........................5 D5
Talbot Place.......................40 F2
Tall Elms Close 4 F4
Tallards Place 37 D4
Tallis Road 3 D1
Tamarisk Mews 10 G4
Tandey Walk 3 C3
Tannery Gardens 19 B6
Tansy Close 7 D6
Tarlton Close.....................13 C1
Tarrington Road 6 F4
Taurus Close 2 F3
Taurus House 27 D3
Taylor House*, Matson Lane
....12 H1
Taylors Ground 10 H3
Teal Close 10 F4
Teasel Close 2 F4
Teddington Gardens 6 G5
Telford Way 15 D1
Temperance Cottages 19 B6
Tempest Drive 37 D1
Temple Close (Glos.) 7 C3
Temple Close (Lydney) 27 D2
Templeway 28 E2
Templeway West ...27 D2/28 E2
Tennyson Avenue 11 C1
Tern Close 7 A5
Terrace, The 23 D4
Tetbury Road.....................11 D4
Tewkesbury Road (Glos.) 2 F3/F5
Tewkesbury Road (Newent)
....36 F4
Thatcham Avenue 11 B4
Theresa Street 5 D4
Thistlebank 2 H3
Thomas Moore Close 4 E1
Thomas Stock Gardens 7 C5
Thomas Street (Chepstow) 37 D2
Thomas Street (Glos.) 16 H5
Thompson Way 3 B3
Thoresby Avenue........11 C4/C5
Thorn Tree Drive*,
   Summer Ho. Lane 38 H3
Thornhill Close 5 C6

Thornwell Road 38 F2/G3
Three Ashes Lane 36 F2
Three Cocks Lane 16 F2
Thrush Close 7 A5
Tibberton Lane 39 C4
Tiberius Avenue 27 C4
Tidswell Close 10 H5
Timber Tump 29 D5
Timmis Close.....................13 A1
Tintern Road 11 D2
Tirley Close 10 G4
Tolsey Gardens 11 B2
Tomlin Place 25 A2
Top Road 35 A4
Tower Close 7 B3
Tower Road 24 H2
Townsend (Mitcheldean) ...40 F2
Townsend (Ruardean) 30 F2
Townsend Close 21 D5
Townsend Cottages*, East St.
....21 C4
Trafalgar Drive.....................3 D1
Trajan Close*, Hadrians Way
....7 D4
Tram Road, The 19 C1
Tramway Road (Ruspidge) 35 A1
Tramway Road (Soudley)
....35 B4/C4
Tredworth Road 6 F4
Trenchard Road 23 B5
Trevone*, Denmark Road ...2 F6
Trevor Road 7 D5
Triangle, The 3 A6
Tribune Place 7 C5
Trier Way 16 F6/H5
Trinity Road (Drybrook) 31 D2
Trinity Road (Glos.) 7 D5
Trinity Way 34 F1/F2
Trubshaw Court...................4 G4
Trygrove 7 B5
Tubular Cottages...............37 C4
Tudor Close 3 D2
Tudor Court 2 G6
Tudor Drive 37 D1
Tudor Street 5 C5
Tudor Walk 17 C3
Tuffley Avenue 5 C5
Tuffley Crescent 5 D6
Tuffley Lane 11 B3/C2
Tufthorn Avenue 19 D3
Tufthorn Close 20 E3
Tufthorn Road 20 E4
Tufthorn Terrace 20 E4
Tufts Cottages 22 H5
Tufts, The 22 H5
Tulworths, The.....................2 H4
Tunacre 9 B1
Turners Close 9 B2
Turnpike Close 37 D1
Turnpike End 38 H5
Turnstile Cottages 30 F2
Turnstone Drive 10 F4
Tusculum Way 40 F2
Tuthill Rise 27 D4
Tutnalls Street 27 D4
Tutshill Gardens 37 C3
Tweenbrook Avenue 6 E5
Twyver Bank 13 D2
Twyver Close.....................13 D3
Tylers Way (Sedbury) 37 D5
Tylers Way (Yorkley) 25 A2
Tyndale Road 8 E3
Tynings Court 4 H4

Tythings Crescent 36 E5
Tythings Mews...................36 F5
Tythings, The.....................36 E5

U

Ullenwood Road 7 B4
Underhill Court*, Underhill Road
....13 A1
Underhill Road....................13 A1
Union Road 18 E6
Union Street 16 H2
Unlawater Lane 35 B5
Uphill Place 5 C6
Uphill Road 29 C5
Upper Bilson Road 34 F2
Upper Church Street 37 D2
Upper Nelson Street 37 D2
Upper Quay House*, Quay St.
....16 E2
Upper Quay Street.............16 F5
Upper Rea*, Rea Lane 5 A6
Upper Road 24 F4
Upper Stowfield Road 29 A2
Upton Close..........................7 C4
Upton Hill 13 B5
Upton Lane 7 D6/12 H6
Upton Street.........................6 F3

V

Valentine Lane 38 H4
Valerian Close 7 C4
Valiant Way 8 G5
Valley Cottages (Upton St. Leo.)
....14 E4
Valley Cottages (Yorkley) .25 A4
Valley Gardens 11 A4
Valley Lane 14 E4
Valley Road (Cinderford) ...34 E4
Valley Road (Lydney)........28 E5
Valley Road (Worrall Hill) ..30 G5
Varley Avenue 8 F5
Varnister 30 H1
Varnister Lane 30 H1
Varnister Road 30 G1
Vauxhall 36 E5
Vauxhall Lane 37 D1
Vauxhall Road (Chepstow) 38 E1
Vauxhall Road (Glos.) 6 F3
Vauxhall Terrace 6 F2
Vensfield Road 10 G3
Vention Lane 29 C3
Verbena Close......................7 C6
Verhonde Place 34 E4
Vernal Close 7 D6
Vertican Road 3 B3
Vervain Close 4 E2
Vestry Gardens 7 A4
Vetch Close 12 G1/H1
Viaduct Villas 29 A3
Viburnum View 7 D6
Vicarage Close (Glos.) 4 G5
Vicarage Close (Lydney) ...28 F3
Vicarage Court 8 H6
Vicarage Lane 8 H6
Vicarage Road 6 G4
Victoria Close 34 E4
Victoria Cottages 10 G2
Victoria Court 2 F3
Victoria Gardens 19 C1
Victoria Road (Chepstow) .38 G3
Victoria Road (Coleford) ...19 C1
Victoria Road (Glos.) 2 F3
Victoria Road (Lydney) 27 D3

Victoria Street (Cinderford)
.............................34 E3/E4
Victoria Street (Glos.) 16 H5
Victoria Vale 34 E3
Victoria Villas 35 B5
Victory Close 4 E1
Victory Road 6 F4
Village, The 39 B2
Villas, The 34 E5
Vincent Avenue 11 C4
Vine Cottages 38 E2
Vine Terrace 2 F6
Vine Tree Cottages 20 F2
Voyce Close 11 D3
Vulcan Way 7 D5
Vyvian Court*, Parliament St.
.............................16 F4

W

Wainland Place 19 B6
Walham Lane 2 E5
Walkers Lane 30 H1
Wallbank House*, Denmark Rd.
.............................2 F6
Walnut Close (Coalway) ...20 F2
Walnut Close (Glos.) 13 B2
Walton Close.......................13 C2
Walwyn Close 40 F3
Ward Avenue 3 C3
Warnless Farm Close 13 D2
Warren Close 4 E2
Warren Slade 38 G3
Warren, The 11 A3
Warwick Avenue 11 C4
Warwick Close 38 F1
Water Meadow 10 G6
Water Wheel Close 10 F4
Waterdale Close 10 F5
Watermans Court 10 F4
Watermead (Brockworth) ...14 H1
Watermead (Lydney)..........27 D3
Watermint Drive...................11 A4
Watermoor Court...................4 F4
Waters Reach 5 B5
Waters Road 38 E2
Waterside Close 10 F4
Waterton Close 8 F5
Waterwells Drive (Glos.) ...11 A6
Waterwells Drive (Hardwicke)
.............................15 D1
Watery Lane (Glos.) 13 D5
Watery Lane (Lydney)........27 D1
Watery Lane (Newent) 36 E6
Watson Grove 7 D6
Watts Close 8 F4
Waverley Road 7 A1
Wayridge, The 13 B1
Weald Close 7 A6
Weavers Road 10 H3
Wedgwood Crescent 34 F2
Wedgwood Drive 3 A4/A5
Weir Bridge Close 7 C3
Well Close*, Summer Ho. Lane
.............................38 H3
Well Cross Road 12 F1
Well House*, High Street ..30 G1
Well Lane.............................31 B2
Welland Road 10 H3
Weller Bungalows 11 C1
Wellesley Street....................6 F5
Wellington Parade 16 H1
Wellington Street................16 G4
Wellmeadow House............23 A6

Wellmeadow Lane..............17 D2
Wells Road 7 A2
Wellsprings Road 2 H6/3 A6
Welsh Street 37 C1
Welveland Lane.....................7 C2
Wendland House................11 A3
Wentworth Close...................2 H4
Wesley Close*, High St. ...28 G1
Wesley Court......................16 H4
Wesley Road 30 H3
Wesley Road (Cinderford) ..34 F2
Wesley Road (Whitecroft) ..24 E4
West Avenue 31 D1
West Bank 29 B3
West End 30 F2
West End Lane 8 F5
West Field 9 B1
West Lodge Drive 7 B4
West View (Lydbrook) 29 C4
West View (Newent) 36 E5
Westbourne Drive 10 G6
Westbury Road 11 D2
Westcote Road 12 E4
Westend Parade 1 C6
Westend Terrace...................1 C6
Westerley Close..................34 F4
Western Avenue (Chepstow)
.............................38 G2
Western Avenue (Mitchdean)
.............................40 F2
Western Cottages 23 B1
Western Way 39 B2
Westfield Avenue 8 H5
Westfield Court 34 F2
Westfield Road (Cinderford)
.............................34 F2
Westfield Road (Glos.) 8 H5
Westfield Terrace 2 E4
Westgate Street 16 E2/F3
Westland Road 10 F6
Westleigh Villas 25 B4
Westmead Road 3 B4
Westminster Court................6 H1
Weston Road 16 F6
Westover Court 4 F2
Westwick Road 39 C4
Wetherleigh Drive 9 B1
Whaddon Place 12 F5
Whaddon Way......................11 D4
Wharfdale Way....................10 F5
Wheatridge Court 7 B6
Wheatridge East, The ..13 C1/C2
Wheatstone, The 13 A1
Wheatstone Road 6 E4
Wheatway 13 B2
Whetstones 35 B5
Whimbrel Road 10 F4
Whimsey Road 31 D6
White Cross Road 28 E3
Whitebeam Close 2 H4
Whitechapel Road 23 B4
Whitecroft Road 23 B4
Whitehill Lane 31 C1
Whiteway Road 12 H1
Whitewell Close 7 C4
Whitfield Street 16 G3
Whitley Court 14 F3
Whittington Walk 36 G5
Whittington Way 23 B6
Whittle Avenue 11 D4
Whitworth Court 11 A6
Whitworth Mews*, Berkeley Cl.
.............................8 G5

Whornes Orchard 13 D2
Widden Street 6 F2
Wigmore Close 7 C5
Wilderness Drive 32 F2
Wildlife Walk 14 H1
Wilkes Avenue 8 E3
Wilkes Meadow 18 F6
Williams Orchard 9 B2
Willow Avenue 6 H4
Willow Close 38 F2
Willow Heights 27 B4
Willow Way 6 H4
Willowcroft Close 13 B2
Willowdean 34 E2
Willowleaze 3 B6
Willows, The (Dymock) 39 B2
Willows, The (Kingsholm) 2 F6
Willows, The (Quedgeley) ..10 G4
Wilton Close 5 D5
Wilton Road 5 D5
Winchcombe Road 12 E3
Winchester Drive 12 E2
Windermere Road 3 A5
Windfall Way 7 A1
Windmill Cottages 6 G2
Windmill Field 7 B4
Windmill Parade 6 G2
Windrush Road 12 E3
Windsor Drive (Glos.) ...11 C3/C4
Windsor Drive (Lydney) 27 A4
Winfield 36 F5
Winneycroft Cottages 13 B3
Winnycroft Lane 12 H5
Winsley Court*, Winsley Road
.............................13 A1
Winsley Road..............13 A1/A2
Winslow Place 4 F3
Winston Road 4 F4
Wintlers Hill 32 H6
Wintles Close 40 F3
Wintour Close 37 C1
Wirewood Close 37 B3
Wirewood Crescent 37 B4
Wishford Close 3 C5
Wisteria Way 4 E2
Withy Mews 6 H6
Woburn Avenue 11 C4
Wolseley Lodge*, Barnwood Rd.
.............................7 A1
Wolseley Road 7 A1
Wood Edge Road 20 E5
Wood Mews...........................1 A5
Wood Road 18 F5
Wood View 34 F3
Woodbine Close 7 C6
Woodcock Close 7 A6
Woodcote 2 H4
Woodcroft Close 37 A4
Woodcroft Lane 37 A4
Woodcroft Terrace 37 A5
Woodend Close 7 C3
Woodend Road 31 D3
Woodford Court 6 H4
Woodgate Close 7 C3
Woodgate Road (Cinderford)
.............................34 F2
Woodgate Road (Mile End) 18 E4
Woodland Close 26 E2
Woodland Green 13 C2
Woodland Place 25 A2
Woodland Rise (Lydney) 27 C3
Woodland Rise (Parkend) ..24 F1
Woodland Road (Bream)....23 A4

Woodland Road (Coleford) 17 B1
Woodland Road (Drybrook)31 D1
Woodland Road (Parkend) 24 F1
Woodland View (Lydbrook) 29 C4
Woodland View (Ruspidge) 35 A1
Woodland Villas 20 F1
Woodlands Close 23 D4
Woodlands Park 10 F4
Woodlands Reach 34 F3
Woodleigh Field 9 B1
Woodpecker Road................5 C6
Woodrow Way 11 A2
Woodruff Close 12 H1
Woods Orchard 12 E3
Woods Orchard Road 12 E3
Woodside Avenue 34 F4
Woodside Cottages 23 B5
Woodside Street 34 F3
Woodvale 11 A4/A5
Woodview 24 H2
Woodville Avenue 18 F5
Woodville Road 34 G3
Woodville Road West 34 F3
Woolstrop House*, St. James
.............................10 H4
Woolstrop Way 11 A2
Worcester Parade 16 H2
Worcester Road 34 G2
Worcester Street 16 G2/G3
Worcester Walk (Broadwell)
.............................18 F6
Worcester Walk (Lydbrook)
.......................29 C6/30 E6
Wotton Court 7 B2
Wotton Elms Court 6 H1
Wotton House*, Horton Rd...6 G2
Wotton Lodge Villas 6 F1
Wren Close 6 H5
Wren Terrace.........................3 B3
Wye Court 29 B3
Wye Crescent 38 E2
Wye Valley Link Road 38 F1
Wye View Road 29 B4
Wyebank Avenue 37 D4
Wyebank Close 37 D4
Wyebank Crescent 37 D4
Wyebank Drive 37 D4
Wyebank Place 37 D4
Wyebank Rise 37 D4
Wyebank Road 37 D4/38 E4
Wyebank View.....................37 D4
Wyebank Way 38 E4
Wyedean Close 28 E5
Wynols Close 20 F1
Wynols Court 20 F1
Wynols Hill Lane 17 D6
Wynols Road 20 F1
Wyntours Parade................28 E3

Y

Yarrow Close.......................12 G1
Yetts, The 38 E5
Yew Tree Cottages
(Up. Lydbrook) 29 D6
Yew Tree Cottages
(Upton St. Leo.) 13 C3
Yew Tree Cottages (Bream)
.............................22 H5
Yew Tree Cottages (Hardwicke)
.............................15 D1
Yew Tree Way.......................3 D4
Yewtree Cottages (Horsley)
.............................29 D4

York Road (Cinderford) **34** G2/G3
York Road (Glos.) **7** A3
York Villas **6** G1
Yorkley Court.....................**24** H4
Yorkley Lane **24** H3
Yorkley Wood **24** G4
Yorkley Wood Road **24** G3
Youngs Orchard **7** B5

Z

Zinnia Close **3** D2
Zion Apartments **17** D4
Zoons Court...........................**8** E1
Zoons Road............................**8** E3

HOSPITALS

Gloucestershire Royal Hospital
....**6** G1
Lydney and District Hospital
....**27** D2
Dike Memorial Hospital **33** C5
Chepstow Community Hospital
....**37** D1

POLICE STATIONS

Barton (Glos.) Police Station
....**6** G3
Bearland (Glos.) Police Station
....**5** D1
Chepstow Police Station **37** D2
Cinderford Police Station....**34** F2
Coleford Police Station **19** D1
Hucclecote Police Station **8** H5
Innsworth Police Station **4** E3
Quedgeley Police Station ..**10** H4
Tutshill Police Station **37** B3

TOURIST INFORMATION CENTRES

Gloucester TIC
   Tel. 01452 396572 ......**16** F3
Coleford TIC
   Tel. 01594 812388 ......**19** C1
Chepstow TIC
   Tel. 01291 623772 ......**37** C3

SCHOOLS & COLLEGES

Abbeymead Prim. School **7** D6
Ann Cam Prim. School **39** B2
Army Apprentices College..**38** H5
Barnwood Park Art College ..**7** B3
Barnwood Prim. School........**7** B2
Beaufort Community School
....**11** B3
Beech Green Prim. School **10** H4
Berry Hill Prim. School **17** D3
Blakeney Prim. School **26** G3
Bream Primary School........**23** A4
Calton Inf. & Jun. Schools **6** E6
Central Technical College **6** H6
Chepstow Comp. School **37** B1
Chosen Hill School **4** H4
Churchdown School..............**4** F4
Churchdown Village Inf. & Jun.
Schools.........................**4** G4
Clearwell Prim. School **21** C1
Coalway Inf. & Jun. Schools
....**20** F1

Coney Hill Community Prim. Sch.
....**7** A4
Crypt School, The **11** D1
Dell Primary School............**37** D2
Dene Magna School **32** H1
Dinglewell Inf. & Jun. Schools
....**7** D4
Drybrook Primary School ..**31** C2
Ellwood Primary School......**20** F6
Elmbridge Infants School......**7** A1
Elmbridge Junior School **7** A1
Field Court Inf. & Jun. Schools
....**10** H5
Finlay Community School **6** G5
Forest View Prim. School ..**34** G2
Glebe Infants School **36** F4
Gloucester College of Art **6** E2
Gloucester Technical College
....**16** F4
Grange Primary School......**11** C2
Grange Infants School.......**11** C3
Hardwicke Prim. School **15** C1
Harewood Inf. & Jun. Schools
....**11** C3
Hatherley Infants School......**6** G4
Hempsted Primary School....**5** A4
Heron Primary School, The .**7** B6
Heywood Community School,
The **34** G1
High School for Girls **2** F6
Highnam Primary School......**9** B1
Hillview Primary School........**7** D3
Huntley School **39** A4
Innsworth Junior School **3** B3
Islamic Girls School **6** F2
Joy's Green Prim. School ..**29** C4
King's School, The **16** G2
Kingsholm Prim. School **16** H1
Lakers School **18** E4
Larkfield Infants School........**3** C3
Linden Primary School.........**5** D5
Littledean Primary School .**34** H3
Longlevens Infants School ..**3** B5
Longlevens Junior School **3** A5
Lydbrook Primary School ..**29** C6
Lydney Primary School......**27** D3
Meadowside Prim. School..**10** H3
Milestone School, The..........**2** H4
Mitcheldean Prim. School ..**40** F3
Moat Primary School, The
....**12** H1
Newent Community Sch. ...**36** E6
Newnham St. Peter's Prim. Sch.
....**35** B5
Offa's Mead Prim. School ..**37** D4
Bishops' College **2** G5
Churchdown Parton Manor
Inf. & Jun. Schools **4** F3
Pembroke Primary School .**38** F2
Picklenash Jun. School **36** E4
Pillowell Community Prim. Sch.
....**24** H4
Primrose Hill Prim. School..**27** B4
Ribston Hall High School......**6** E6
Robinswood Prim. School ..**13** A2
Royal Forest of Dean College,
The **18** E3
Ruardean Primary School ..**30** F2
Woodside Primary School..**30** H5
Severn Vale School............**10** G4
Severnbanks Prim. School **27** D5
Sir Thomas Rich's Sch. **3** B6
Soudley Primary School **35** B3

St. Anthony's Convent School
....**34** F3
St. Briavels Prim. School....**21** C5
St. James Junior School **6** F3
St. John's Primary School ..**19** B1
St. John's-on-the-Hill School
....**37** C3
St. Mary's R.C. Inf. & Jun. Schs.
....**38** E2
St. Mary's Primary School....**3** D3
St. Paul's Primary School ..**16** F6
St. Peter's High School **12** E4
St. Peter's Primary School ..**6** H1
St. Whites School **34** F5
Staunton & Corse Prim. School
....**40** G5
Steam Mills Prim. School ..**31** D5
Thornwell Primary School ..**38** G3
Tredworth Infants School......**6** F4
Tredworth Junior School **6** F4
Tuffley Primary School **12** E4
Tutshill Primary School **37** A3
Twigworth Primary School ..**2** F2
University of Gloucestershire
....**2** H6
Upton St. Leonards Prim. School
....**13** D2
Westbury-on-Severn Prim. Sch. ..
....**32** G6
Whitecross School.............**28** E2
Widden Primary School.......**6** F2
Wyedean School **37** D4
Wynstones School **12** E5
Yorkley Primary School.....**24** H3

INDUSTRIAL ESTATES

125 Business Park **5** C3
....**5** B3
Abenhall Technology Centre
....**40** G3
Anson Business Park **4** H1
Ashville Business Park **4** F1
Ashville Industrial Estate **5** C6
Barnwood Bus. Centre **7** C2
Barrett Industrial Estate........**1** D6
Bulwark Ind. Estate **38** F3
Capitol Park.......................**11** B1
Cattle Market Ind. Estate **2** E5
Central Trading Estate.......**11** B2
Centurians Bus. Park **5** C6
Charles Street Ind. Area **6** F2
Cinderford Enterprise Centre
....**34** E1
Cleeve Mill Business Park..**36** H4
Corinium Business Park **31** D6
Cotswold Edge Business Park
Eastbrook Road Trading Estate
....**7** A3
Eastern Avenue Retail Park **6** H3
Eastern Avenue Trading Estate
....**6** H3
Forest Vale Ind. Estate **33** D2
Francis Woodcock Trading Est.
....**6** G3
Glevum Works Trading Estate
....**6** F4
Gloucester Business Park..**10** G5
Gloucester Retail Park........**7** A3
Goodridge Trading Estate ..**11** A2
Green Farm Bus. Park **10** H3
Holyhill Park **33** D2

Innsworth Technology Park ..**3** A2
Io Centre **14** G1
Ladygrove Business Park ..**40** H3
Lancaster Centre.................**4** G1
Llanthony Ind. Estate...........**5** C2
Lydney Ind. Estate **28** G6
Madleaze Ind. Est. **5** D3/16 E6
Meteor Business Park..........**4** G1
Mews Enterprise Workshops
....**40** F2
Mill Lane Ind. Estate **37** D3
Mill Place Trading Estate (North)
....**5** C4
Mill Place Trading Estate (South)
....**5** C4
Monk Meadow Trading Estate
....**5** C4
Morelands Trading Estate ..**16** F6
Mushet Industrial Park........**19** D2
Olympus Park Business Centre
....**11** A2
Pavilion Business Park **31** D6
Pegasus Building...............**11** A3
Perry Centre, The **15** D1
Princess Royal Ind. Est. **23** C4
Prospect Works **7** A3
Pullman Business Centre **6** F1
Quedgeley Distribution Centre
....**15** D1
Quedgeley Enterprise Centre
Site No 5 ....**11** C5
Quedgeley Enterprise Centre
HQ..............................**11** A5
Quedgeley Enterprise Centre
Site No 1 ....**11** B4
Quedgeley Enterprise Centre
Site No 7 ....**11** B5
Quedgeley Trading Estate West
....**15** B2
School Hill Trading Estate ..**37** D2
Severnside Trading Estate ..**5** B2
St. James Trading Estate **6** G3
St. Oswalds Retail Park.......**1** D5
Station Yard Ind. Estate **37** D3
Staunton Court Bus. Park .**40** E5
Steadings Business Centre, The
....**1** A1
Stenders Bus. Centre **40** E2
Sudbrook Trading Estate...**16** E5
Tuffley Trading Estate **11** B1
Tufthorn Ind. Estate **20** E3
Unit Athena **11** A3
Units Apollo **11** A3
Vantage Point Bus. Village
....**40** F2
Venture Business Centre **5** D3
Waterwells Business Park ..**11** A6